STONE & WATER

*Walking the Spiritual Variant of the
Camino Portuguese*

Roy Uprichard

Cover image shows a sixteenth-century statue of St James, on Mount Santiaguino, Padron, Galicia.

Route of the Spiritual Variant of the Camino Portuguese

Table of Contents

Preface

Apart from being a pleasurable route to Santiago on the Portuguese Way, 'Spiritual Variant' is a good metaphor to describe the range of experiences pilgrims may have on their journey.

Walking as a pilgrim is a *variation* on the typical holiday. Indeed, this experience pushes everyone to *vary* their lifestyle, demanding a change of daily habits and routine; a reformulation of priorities that encourages a deeper connection with the wonder of nature and with ourselves. For human beings are multi-layered, constantly evolving, different and *various*.

The very richness of humanity springs out of our *variety*, our diversity. Our task is to embrace and celebrate these differences. Maybe this is the essential *spirit* of walking The Way, the energy pushing from below with its special and unique thrill. Maybe this is why, as Roy writes, this experience is not about gaining a Compostela.

I hope that you too may experience some of the San Ero-like moments of peace and connection that Roy describes in Armenteira on the Stone and Water route, on Mount Santiaguino, or along the way.

My passion has been to build a network of official hostels where pilgrims will find welcoming shelter on the Portuguese Way and on the Spiritual Variant. So I can only feel grateful to Roy who has written such a vivid report of his experiences and of the hospitality he received.

Buen Camino to everyone!

Celestino Lores
President of the Friends of the Camino Portuguese

Introduction

In August 2016 I walked north from Porto on the Camino Portuguese, to Santiago de Compostela.

The route that made the deepest impression came just after Pontevedra: The Spiritual Variant, or Stone and Water route, which was added to the Camino itinerary in 2013.

Its meditative paths led me through a region of lavish fertility; of vineyards and green pastures; of forested hillsides, remote glens and living waters. By following it, I discovered a place of history, myth and Celtic resonance with Ireland.

I offer these words from a desire to share something of its wonder and so that you, too, might be tempted to walk its paths.

Chapter 1

Preparations

August 2016. Bangor, Co. Down.

While preparing for my Camino this summer, I'd read some of mythologist Joseph Campbell's work. Rather than seeking a meaning for life, he believed that we sought to 'feel the rapture of being alive.'

I knew what he meant. In 2014 I had discovered some of that rapture through the intensity of the Camino experience, making the return to the commonplace more difficult. For though I left the Camino, it never left me, resonating now in every woodland path of home, walking me back to an almost Celtic reconnection with nature.

And now, two years later, this benign addiction has resurfaced in my desire to feel again the crunch of boots on gravel and to breathe the scent of fresh morning air far beyond my office window.

I also know that the physical effort of walking long days can tune out much of my internal chatter, running down my mind's meter, until its ticker-tape commentary stutters to a halt before an occasional field of dreams.

Perhaps I need this reboot more than ever now, as Britain walks away from European friends. Maybe I want to walk in the opposite direction, reminding myself of what unites us – our shared heritage along the very paths where the idea of Europe was born, paths trod by people from all nations united in a common challenge, and looking for and beyond a city on a hill.

* * *

Yesterday I drove past where I'd once lived, in Dundela, East Belfast, our garden backing on to where C. S. Lewis was born. Close by, in St Mark's Anglican Church on the Holywood Road, where his grandfather had been rector, Lewis had commissioned a stained glass triptych of saints as a memorial to his father, with James central. I remember in the 1980s staring at the images underneath his feet, wondering what they meant, not yet knowing that scallop shell, purse, and staff symbolised the historic Santiago Pilgrimage. Back then, the Pilgrimage seemed an arcane, medieval memory. No one could have foreseen its resurgence.

*The Lewis Window in St Marks Belfast, with the Santiago
symbols at his feet and the Translatio galleon top right*

So I stood again before the Lewis window, gazing at its sunlit kaleidoscope of colours and thinking, how appropriate that a medieval scholar should re-present the same symbols that appear everywhere along the Camino routes. Perhaps Lewis was suggesting we were all part of one another, and that in a divided Europe we needed our differing strands.

This time, though, my eye was drawn to just above James' left shoulder, to a small medieval galleon, its sail billowing, as if a prototype for Lewis's *The Dawn Treader*. That may be true, but its original purpose was to complete the tableaux of the James legend, representing his final voyage, back to Galicia.[1]

Then through the silence, the realisation that in just over a week I would step onto a launch at Vilanova and travel the last lap of that mythic sea route.

* * *

But tonight it's late. I'm nervous and excited. Lying open on my desk are the journals of the scholar-

---

[1] Tradition says that sometime after AD33 James journeyed to preach in Spain. On his return to Jerusalem in AD44, he was beheaded on the orders of Herod Agrippa. Legend records the sea-borne return of the remains of St James to Galicia, in a journey known as the Transfer (*Translatio*) back to his missionary heartland.

monk, Martin Sarmiento, an eighteenth-century pilgrim to Santiago, and part inspiration for the Spiritual Variant.

I unfold a map of one of his circuits through south-west Galicia, then trace out a line, pronouncing the names of Poio, Combarro, Armenteira and Vilanova de Arousa. I hope that the Stone and Water route might feel like a Camino from twenty years ago when the hiss of sickles and the slap of fresh yellow paint welcomed new generations of pilgrims to its ancient paths.

One last time I play a video of the Stone and Water route, its lingering shots of abandoned water mills and remote monasteries accompanied by a soundtrack of reels as if from the West of Ireland.

The screen darkens. I turn off my laptop, fold the map back into the text, place my rucksack in the hall, and climb the stairs to try to sleep. Even a little.

Chapter 2

Porto to Pontevedra

From Porto, it's been a week of stifling heat for the ripples of pilgrims following blue arrows south, to Fatima, or yellow arrows north, to Santiago. We sauntered through river valleys exploding with vines and corn or over sparkling cobbled granite past white churches with tiled fronts and bulbous bell towers. Barcelos and Ponte de Lima had vivid yellow, and red umbrellas strung high across their streets, as if a flock of Mary Poppinses had blown in on the east wind.

Climbs and meandering descents followed through timeless hamlets, past millraces, over pristine earthen tracks, ancient stone paths or Roman roads, and through the ubiquity of eucalyptus forests, to here, late afternoon before the Porta do Camino, the entrance point to Pontevedra's historic centre.

I've arranged to meet some of my walking companions at seven p.m. for a pilgrim's menu:

Thomas, from Limerick, Jim and Judith from Canada, and their Estonian friend, Maija. But first, I need to visit the Tourist Office before it closes, to learn more about the Spiritual Variant.

The Office has an A5 fold-out leaflet outlining its three stages. Stage one (20 kilometres) is to Poio, Combarro then into the mountains to the monastery village of Armenteira. Stage two covers the twenty-four kilometres of the 'Stone and Water' route to the Arousa estuary and Vilanova. The final phase is by boat, twenty-eight kilometres on the Ruta Maritima, the Translatio route to Pontesecures.

I tell the tourist officer that on this Camino I am not collecting *credencial* stamps every day to earn a Compostela certificate from Santiago Cathedral. 'But for those who want to earn a Compostela, does the Spiritual Variant count?'

'Oh yes,' he tells me, 'but not in itself. Pilgrims need to start at least at Tui or Redondela to reach the minimum 100 kilometres. If they begin in Galicia, they should collect two stamps each day. When they present their *credencials* at the cathedral, they should tell the official they have taken the Spiritual Variant option.'

He then rummages through drawers and finds leaflets in English on the Monasteries of Poio and Armenteira. 'I have this book also,' he says, 'about Padre Martin Sarmiento's connections with

Pontevedra – but only in the Galician tongue, Gallego.'

It contains directions to the Sarmiento family home, which is close by. I thank him, place the leaflets and book in my pack and walk through bustling streets to the *Praza de Mendes Nunez*, its balconies' window boxes overflowing with colour.

I take a seat in the café and read through some notes on Sarmiento's exceptional life, his name inextricably linked with the Spiritual Variant, Galician culture and language.

Born in Villafranca del Bierzo in 1695 as Pedro Jose Garcia Balboa, his family moved a few months later to Pontevedra. At fifteen years old, he joined the Benedictine order in Madrid, taking the name of Martin Sarmiento.

He soon revealed himself as a polymath with a ravenous interest not only in theology but botany, literature, medicine, linguistics and ethnography. Away from his library, he recharged his energies through walking, entranced by the beauty of the natural world. In 1745, he took a really long walk, combining pilgrimage and field trip on his journey north from Madrid to Santiago, where he collected a plenary indulgence.[1]

---

[1] Indulgences were based on the notion of the 'Year of Jubilee' edict in Leviticus, which discharged debts. The Christian appropriation of this seems to have begun with Isidore of Seville

From reading his journals, I believe he was partly motivated by a passion for collecting words, plants, and routes – a pilgrim to knowledge as well as to Santiago. On the way, and on his further wanderings through Galicia, he found a trove of cultural treasures, in its language, folk tales and songs, and the God in all things, as the natural world was, for him, a world of wonder.

In 1754, he returned to Pontevedra, and from here set out on walking circuits west and north, to further document Galicia's language, culture, and topography.

Tomorrow I will follow in his footsteps to the Monastery of Poio.

But for now, I walk back through a street where the aroma of fresh, charcoal-grilled Langoustines smokes out from a restaurant to wrap itself around me. My steps slow past pavement tables filled with plates of fan-shaped shells, steamed open to reveal their yellow and white contents, garnished with onions and peppers. Scallop shells everywhere –

560-636, offering partial indulgences based on the possibility of earning, through prayer and good works, a year's remission from purgatorial punishment for sins – a sort of time-off for good behaviour. Even better, a plenary (or in Sarmiento's case) a Jubilee indulgence could completely eradicate time in purgatory – a get-out-of-jail-free-card. These were first granted to pilgrims journeying to the Holy Land, then to those involved in the struggle against the Moors in Spain.

underfoot, set into walls and on restaurant tables. Shaking off this aromatic enchantment, I hurry to meet the others.

We sit down together for a pilgrim's menu, in a side street restaurant, for courses of salad, hake or chicken, pasta and *patatas bravas* – carbs for the journey, washed down by sharp red wine. Thomas just has water. I ask him how he first heard of the Camino, as he like me is a repeat offender.

'It was just three years ago, at a family wedding. Some of the guests were sharing their stories of walking. Then I saw the film *The Way*, and that clinched it.'

'Martin Sheen,' I say, 'is responsible for so many blisters.'

He nods. 'It's strange. Back home after an hour's walking, I'm bored, but here I can walk all day.'

Thomas's introduction to the Camino, like mine, began with the final sections of the Camino Frances, from Sarria to Santiago.

'That was two years ago this September, my wife and I walking. She thought it was OK; I loved it and couldn't wait to get back. So, last year I took a month off to walk from Logrono to Santiago. My wife said, 'What's going on? That's something students do on a gap year.''

'Yes, before they graduate to work in the service sector,' I say.

'I didn't have the words to explain to her. Just that I had to do it. And I didn't know why.'

'But you did when you got there?'

He nods and continues. 'Then this April, to complete it, I walked from the start, at St Jean. And now, the Camino Portuguese. My wife asked me, 'Again? That's April and now August.' I promised her, just the two weeks, from Porto. And that this will be the last for a while. But I just had to be here.' He faces me with his shoulders hunched, his palms upturned as if in mitigation.

'It just clears my mind. For most people, a mid-life crisis means an affair or a sports car, but, *this* is my affair.'

'Sometimes you just have to go over the wall,' I say.

'Aye. Better than going up it! Maybe this time I'll get it out of my system.'

I look at him and wonder if he, or I, ever will.

Judith and Jim are from Toronto. 'We have such busy lives,' Judith says. 'With our separate careers, we hardly saw each other. We needed this.'

Judith walked the Camino Frances two years ago. 'If I hadn't gone I think I don't know what would have happened. With all the pressures of kids, parents and work. And I walked with people who seemed to have the same experience as me, with their family. Incredible.'

Jim at first didn't understand why Judith was so enthusiastic about the Camino. 'But I'm beginning to see the attractions,' he adds. 'For me, last year got a bit intense. I had some difficulties with business partners. The usual stuff. I'm glad we chose the Portuguese route. It's much quieter than the Camino Frances, Judith says. It's given us more time to talk things through. We've made plans to scale back on commitments when we get back home.'

'And it's such a spiritual experience as well,' Judith adds. 'I never do church at home anymore. But here, I look for the credential stamps that you get in churches. It makes it feel of more value somehow. I like sitting in all these little churches, in the cool and the quiet. It gives you time to think.'

As the waiter arrives with more red wine, Thomas confesses that earlier, he went to Mass. 'I went last night as well.' He shakes his head. 'I never go when I'm at home.'

He looks bewildered. 'It's like that U2 song, 'I still haven't found what I'm looking for.''

'That's our favourite U2 track,' Judith says, leaning across, squeezing his hand.

'All your buses are coming at once,' I say to Thomas. 'Have you heard of St Cormac of the Sea?'

'Yes. Vaguely. From around the time of Columba?'

'That's him,' I say. 'He was one of our Celtic Monks, our Peregrinati, setting out in coracles on missions of discovery, in search of a place to preach or pray. Columba's advice was 'Let your feet follow your heart until you find the place of your resurrection.''

'Cormac tried and failed three times. Maybe he couldn't fit in with Columba's strict regime. But on his fourth journey, he found the place he was looking for. You're like him.'

As perhaps am I.

Thomas looks at me, quizzically. 'What's your job at home, Roy?'

'I was a teacher, in a Further Education College. Now retired.'

'I thought so. Either that or a priest.'

I laugh. 'I'm Anglican. Still practising. Maybe someday I'll get it right. My family are very traditional Protestants. They'd be amused that I was taken for a priest. It would confirm all their suspicions that I was going soft, deserting the old ways.'

It's strange, I thought, that I'm the only one who attends church fairly regularly at home but never here, except for the pilgrim's Mass at the end of a Camino. The churches here, large or small, rarely move me. Rather, it's out on the track, walking through nature, when a landscape comes into focus and overwhelms me with its beauty. Or a sudden awareness that millions over the centuries have trod the same path. That moves me the most.

But then Maija, from Estonia, speaks. She spent most of the evening smiling, nodding, perhaps only understanding some of what we said. But I'm wrong. In halting English, she says, 'The Santiago Pilgrimage is very popular in my country. Two years ago I walked from Santiago to Finisterre. I got my Compostela and took it home. My mother was so proud that she framed it. It's on the wall of our flat, at home. And now this year, I've walked from Porto,' she smiles, shaking her head as if in disbelief. 'I saved my holidays up for this. It's so wonderful to be outside in this sunshine. I work in an office all year round. Stuck inside. And now, in four years' time, it's my new dream to walk all of the Santiago Way across Spain. Yes, my dream.'

Tonight we will separate, they walking on to Caldes de Reyes, then Padron, and me, veering off on the Spiritual Variant. I will miss them. But at least I know I will stay with friends of a friend, Alfonso and Debee Cherene, who have moved from Madrid to Vilanova de Arousa, opening their house to pilgrims.

Later I say to Thomas, 'If you have time, you should visit Muxia and enjoy a couple of days on the coast.' We exchange mobile numbers and plan to meet again in Santiago. It turns out we are on the same flight home, to Dublin.

Chapter 3

Pontevedra and Poio

In the morning I say goodbye to my companions and enjoy a leisurely breakfast then walk through busy streets to the route's starting point, the eighteenth-century Baroque masterpiece, the Capella La Peregrina.

A spiral stone staircase leads to the best view of its unique floor plan – in the shape of a scallop shell. The altar's centrepiece, a recessed statue of the Virgin, looks like a giant porcelain doll become a medieval pilgrim. In her right hand, she holds a staff with a mini-gourd attached, while in her left is the infant Jesus, clothed in white, as if ready for a christening. A Napoleonic-style bicorne hat and delicate gold lace sky-blue robe complete her wardrobe, one fit more for grand interiors rather than dusty tracks.

Above them, three winged cherubs surround a post-advent scene as, with Joseph's support, the holy family leaves Bethlehem. Below me, five people kneel in prayer. All is quiet until a tour arrives to break the silence.

Ara Peregrina Church Pontevedra, the route's starting point, its floor plan in the shape of a scallop shell

I descend La Peregrina's stone staircase and out into the buttery sunshine, seeking the Camino Portuguese symbols – brass scallop-shell designs inlaid every few metres into the smooth stone. They lead me again through the old quarter, a twin of Santiago but without its rows of souvenir shops. I stroll through a maze of streets connecting four exquisite Renaissance squares of arcaded mansions, elegant wrought-iron balconies and sandstone colonnades.

A classical guitarist plays Cavatina. Outside the same restaurant as last night, a woman chalks up its seafood delicacies. A man shakes out a tablecloth of brilliant white, to settle on a rustic wooden table. A new day.

I walk on to the *Rio Leriz* and its seventeenth-century *Puente del Burgo*. Students, office workers, and pilgrims mingle, loosing a Babel of languages that drift in the humid air – Pontevedra's new normal. For the next two kilometres, the arrows take me through narrowing suburban streets and onto a minor road tracking the railway line.

Just before the Camino Portuguese turns right, at a railway underpass, a large rectangular sign announces, off to the left, the beginning of the *Variante Espiritual Del Camino Portugues a Santiago*. The sign's vertical line is broken by towns, villages and kilometres between. Below it another sign, in vivid yellow and blue, shows the elevation and distances covered on its three stages.

Turning left here on the Spiritual Variant

As two walkers pass, wishing me a *Buen Camino* on their way to Caldas del Reyes, I turn left and cross a bridge over the A9. Soon, the first of many *Variante*

Espiritual staked markers – rectangular wooden signs with a recessed yellow arrow and a Santiago cross overlaid by a scallop shell. Signs and arrows lead me underneath the A9, to again rise on an earthen path between fields of vines and corn.

A typical sign on the Spiritual Variant

As I saunter along, lost in delight, a young female pilgrim powers past me, with a wave and a 'Buen Camino.' But she has missed a turn to the right, onto a steep track, almost overgrown. I shout out to her and point in the right direction. She retraces her steps, stops with me for a moment, removes her pack and downs a long draught from her water bottle, a sheen of sweat on her forehead, her brown hair in tight curls, reminding me of my daughter.

She arrived on Saturday and didn't know it was

a Portuguese festival weekend. 'Lots of people were running around naked. Not very spiritual. But apart from that, I liked the coastal route from Porto. Very isolated.'

'You'll like this route then,' I tell her.

'You know you're on the Camino on a day like this,' she says, 'when strangers shout after you, but it's to tell you that you're going in the wrong direction.'

'Yes. In a land where wine is cheaper than water … and you don't believe you've only walked 5k to get here.'

'Then you realise that Spanish kilometres are longer.' She smiles. 'But also …' she says, looking around, 'that you never want *this* to end.'

With that, she hoists her pack, and we walk on together for a little. Hanna is from Rothenburg, a small town in Southern Germany. 'Few have heard of it, but it's part of what's known as *The Romantic Road* through Bavaria. Full of medieval towns.' Her English is perfect, without even a hint of an accent.

'I suppose this is also a road of romance,' I say. I ask her how she heard of the Camino, and this route.

'Well, there were scallop shells motifs on a house close to where we lived. I thought they were just decorative, but my mother said they were something to do with travel. Then in University, I took a module on Medieval History, learnt about James, and the pilgrimage phenomenon.'

Friends of hers had walked the Camino Frances, 'but I wanted to walk somewhere different, quieter.'

She came across an article in a walking magazine about the Camino Portuguese, and the Spiritual Variant, which to her seemed perfect.

'The idea for this route, it's like an act of faith I think, a bit like in that Kevin Costner film, *Field of Dreams*, that 'If you build it they will come.''

She says it was one of her father's favourite films.

'And one of mine also,' I say.

She is silent for a moment.

I smile. 'I think more will walk this section.'

'Do you?' she asks.

'Yes, this thing is growing each year and pilgrims will want to see new routes, new landscapes, with a spiritual resonance.'

Hanna tells me she has just finished a Theology and History degree and is taking a year off to decide what to do next. Perhaps teaching, she says, without great enthusiasm.

As she started very early this morning, her target today is Poio's Monastry. She says she wants to spend some time there. I wonder if she is considering a calling. I tell her that I want to walk on to Combarro and from there start the climb to Armenteira in the morning.

Hanna walks too fast for me. I tell her that I need to stop for a breather and send her on ahead. With a wave she is soon back in power-walking mode, her footsteps swallowed by soft soughing wind through the trees.

I continue at my more sedate pace. In August I attended a retreat in Lindisfarne, Northumbria, and came across a quote by Thich Nhat Hahn, saying, 'Although we walk all the time, our walking is more like running. When we walk like that, we print anxiety and sorrow on the Earth. We have to walk in a way that we only print peace on the Earth.'

It's been a while since my walking was like running, but he's not wrong. I pass a field of corn nine feet high, its wind- swayed leaves stirred into an applause like soft rain on rooftops. And I'm grateful there are still such paths through nature on which to practice this more leisurely walking.

The track emerges behind the mottled granite of *Campano's Igrexa de San Pedro*, its origins in the fourteenth century. A presentation board explains that *Petroglificas* (spiral circles carved into stone) were found nearby, dated from four thousand years ago.

Evidence of Galician fondness for stone circles is everywhere, their traditional dwellings, round-houses circled in settlements (castros). Circles were significant for all Celts, symbolising the sun's journey, or the seasons turning. And also for Irish and British Celtic Christians, who adorned their crosses with a superimposed circle, now evolved to represent eternal life.

The village slumbers deep in siesta curfew, except for one elderly man in a threadbare black suit slowly pushing his bike through thick heat, his creaking wheel counterpoint to a cicada's trill – the sound of endless summer over golden fields.

The road narrows to an earthen track weaving through a timeless eucalyptus wood. Underfoot, last year's dead-leaf litter lies crunchy, while occasional gusts of wind blow through the leaves. Their crisp minty pine scent, like incense, fills the air, just as it did in the time of Galicia's prolonged isolation beyond the mountain palisade of the *Cordillera Cantabricas*.

I stop, remove my pack, devour the remains of this morning's chorizo baguette, and drain my water bottle before resuming the walk. For the next kilometre, the path snakes through the wood, which slowly returns me to the present, with tarmac, with gentrified gated houses and high above, with an aeroplane's whine.

Shortly after, I catch my first sight of glinting blue water, the beginnings of the *Ria de Pontevedra*, flowing around the *Isla de Tambo* and its pleasure armada of small yachts and launches.

The road widens. Left at the next roundabout is the Monastery of St John de Poio. Imposing. Austere. Thirty plane trees shade its south-western side, bringing relief from the late afternoon heat. In their midst, two large Crucerios, prayer stones, stand in a silent summons.

Poio Monastery

I sit for a moment, then circle round to the monastery's north-eastern side, where a record-breaking eighteenth-century Horreo stands – a stretched rectangular stone granary on stilts – one hundred and twenty-three square metres of it. Behind it, an orchard garden of orange, lemon and laurel trees, edged by magenta bougainvillaea and white rhododendron.

I sit on a bench, entranced by the sweet lemony scent and again think of Sarmiento wandering, collecting, compiling.

His journals record that in a garden in this monastery, he recorded his first sight of a lily brought from India, renamed the *Flor de Santiago* because of its red and white colouring and its design (similar to the Santiago Cross) adding its features to his burgeoning Galician *Encyclopaedia Botanica*.

Though intending to walk on to Combarro, I pause at this place of deep silences. I decide to book in tonight behind these thick granite walls that preserve the memory of sequestered lives, ordered by the liturgy of the hours.

After making my request to the woman at reception, she replies in hesitant English, 'It is possible.' I provide my details. She runs the back of her fingertips along a line of hooked keys, their metal tags jangling like chimes, stops, selects, and hands me my key.

Wide marble stairs lead to the hostelry, added in 1960 – and its seemingly endless, empty corridors. My room has whitewashed walls, with an icon of the holy family and a print of beached fishing boats beneath flower-strewn verandas. The shuttered windows open to a view over the *Horreo* and the orchard garden.

My reservation entitles me to a complimentary tour, so, an hour later, I walk downstairs, past the café courtyard, and trees with ripe lemons hung like Christmas baubles.

I learn that the original Visigoth Sepulchre became a Benedictine Monastery in the tenth century. In 1837, secularisation ended its writ, and in 1890 the Mercedarians, the Order of Mercy (founded in the thirteenth century to redeem Christian captives from their Muslim captors) re-tasked their mission, transforming the site, first into a psychiatric hospital, and then in 1959, a seminary.

We begin underneath the ornately ribbed Renaissance vaults of the seventeenth-century fountain cloister. In the middle of the monastery yard, a giant palm and camellia trees shade the ornate fountain, its cooling water piped from Mount Castrove, two kilometres away. Set between the yellow casement windows of the upper cloister, sundials cast long shadows. Underfoot are dozens of little crosses etched into the cloister's paving, marking the site of the original parish cemetery.

The church is grandiose Renaissance and Baroque. For one hundred and fifty years, generations of craftsmen refined its opulent high altar with gold leaf.

More prosaically, a workman today applies in circular motion what smells like linseed oil to the mahogany choir stalls. I loiter as its thick aura hangs in the air, the aroma of aged wood, of dark corners in dimly lit churches, of whispered imprecations from lives long past.

For some moments I fail to notice that the tour has moved on. I turn and follow past the splayed arches and balustrades to our final station, before the *Bayeaux Tapestry* of mosaics, the commanding 'Road to Santiago' – two hundred square metres imaging pilgrim traffic, towns and cities, along the way from Paris to Galicia.

At the sun begins to set, I find a bench under the burnished plane trees and read my leaflets on the history and legends associated with Combarro and Armenteira, finding more Celtic connections.

As I walk back towards the hostelry see Hanna again, on a bench in the orchard garden, writing.

She looks up and waves. 'Aah, you stayed. You didn't walk on to Combarro?'

'No. A change of plans. This place caught my attention.'

'It really is quieter on this section of the walk. More meditative,' she says.

I share my Thich Nhat Hahn quote, and she writes it down, then closes her journal, before saying, 'We are really lucky to experience this, before all the others who will come and discover this route. I may stay one more night.'

I nod and say goodnight, walking back to marble corridors, where mine is no longer the only footfall. A group of retired women arrive midst a fever of cushions for embroidery, followed by a troop of upmarket leather clad touring bikers, the decorative chains on their jackets clinking. As the light finally fades, I close the shutters and climb into bed. The last blackbird quietens.

Chapter 4

To Armenteira

Suddenly, at four thirty a.m. I'm wide awake, rested but restless, anxious to get to Combarro and start the climb of Mount Castrove. Outside is a profound silence, which, like darkness, is at its greatest just before dawn.

Thirty minutes later, showered and shod, I descend the marble stairs, startling the night attendant at his computer terminal, return my key and walk out through the courtyard's floodlit sepia. Rumi, St John of the Cross, Thomas Keating, they all say the same thing: silence is the first language of God, all else a poor translation. I listen for a still small whisper, but the only sound comes from my echoing faint footsteps.

An occasional flare of headlights on the Carretera. Beyond, only a sliver of waning moon. An hour later, in the fishing village of Combarro, I walk over damp sand and down to the water's edge. In the faint lamplight, the hull of an upturned dingy resembles the outline of an abandoned coracle. The air is cold, the water as still as a lake. Almost nothing moves, only a man slowly, cautiously lifting litter into his cart. The town is yet to stir.

Tourism has transformed this fishing village, through house conversions into bars or restaurants serving fresh seafood and Albarino wines. I wait on the beach, longing for the first grey of dawn. Across the Ria, an industrial plant starts to rumble then growls like a jet engine. The spell is broken. Giant fans raise clouds of white smoke above dystopian red glows.

As Orion moves into soft focus, I walk through the old quarter. It hosts seven Crucerios, all with a Christ crucified on their front side, facing inland, and Mary at his back, facing out to sea. Together forever. Initially placed at crossroads, their function may have been to Christianise pagan cult places of worship, where witches and the still active *Meigas* gathered.

But other traditions claims they serve as protection against the *Santa Compana* (Holy Company), a procession of souls in purgatorial torment who wander through villages after midnight to announce an impending death. Though the *Santa Compana* is invisible, their presence is said to induce a shiver as they pass. A faint glow of floating candlelight may also occur.

In Ireland, the Banshee serves a similar function – a female spirit whose shrieking or keening announces the death of a family member.[1]

Galicians, like many Irish, are comfortable with the closeness of the Otherworld. But happily, dawn is near, and as I walk along the Pier da Rua, the only visible coven of Meigas are smiling miniatures corralled behind shop windows, and the only candles remain packaged securely on a shelf.

Narrow walkways funnel me past Combarro's unique selling point, its promenade line of thirty *Horreos*, raised high, and now partnered with dozens of gift and craft shops, then bars and restaurants, with their stale beer odours, their pungent rubbish bags.[2]

At seven a.m. and still in darkness, I attempt to trace a route out of the old quarter but get lost. I left Poio far too early. I return and wait until painted arrows are revealed, pointing across the main street, beginning a maze of climbing turns.

A group of early-morning parishioners file into

---

[1] Banshees are associated with the burial mounds in the Irish countryside, populated by the inhabitants of the other world, known as the Sidhe, and where the Tuatha De Danaan retreated after defeat by the Milesians/Gaels.Similarly, in Welsh folklore, the spectral hounds of Cwn Annwn foretell death to any who hear them.

[2] Poio may have the largest Horreo in Galicia, but Combarro the greatest concentration throughout Galicia: sixty of them.

the church. As the chapel bell tower chimes eight times, I turn into the climb.

Finally, the houses thin and the trees thicken. The trunks of tall pines stand burnished red in the morning sun. Interwoven vines, draped across granite posts form covered alleyways, candelabras of light-green grapes hanging down. A single white stallion grazes, then stares. Between caw-calls, silence.

The road meanders past oak, chestnut, then vegetable plots to become the Camino Esperon, gently inclining onto the Camino Vilar, the slopes above dense with ash and eucalyptus. A Crucerio, with Mary in silent gaze, looks back over the Ria.

Two pilgrims gain on me, Ferdie from Düsseldorf and Estevao from Porto. They met three years ago on the Camino and remained friends. Since then, Estevao has volunteered as a hospitalero in the monastery Albergue of Samos and Ferdie has returned to walk different routes. They hope to make it to the summit of Mount Castrove before the sun heats up.

'We know this mountain,' Ferdie says, 'from two years ago.' He makes a steep incline with his hand. 'I've walked a lot in Northern Portugal and Galicia. I just love stepping away from all the demands of daily life.'

Inevitably, they mention Brexit. 'What's happening there?' Ferdie asks.

I apologise, saying Northern Ireland voted to remain. On my last Camino, I tell them, I met so many who were proud of being Spanish *and* European, Irish *and* European, Dutch *and* …

'German *and*,' Ferdie says. 'We still hope Brexit may not happen.'

Ahead, the freshly resurfaced road takes another series of climbing turns, and again the crisp minty pine scent of eucalyptus drifts in to envelop us. A friend to pilgrims as we climb into the mountains.[3]

'Smell that,' I say. We stop to deep breathe.

'The hotter the weather,' Estevao says, 'the stronger the scent released. But we have to be very careful here because eucalyptus is very flammable. It's the leaves, full of oil. So far, this year, we've been lucky.'

Their pace is faster than mine, and I begin to notice what feels like a blister on the inside of my left heel. Eventually, I fall behind and stop. They turn and wait. I point to my foot and shout out, 'A blister. You go on. I'll catch up later.'

---

[3] Eucalyptus was first propagated in Galicia in 1868, from seeds sent from Australia by a Galician expatriate Benedictine monk. But it remains a controversial, fast growing tree which drains the soil of nutrients.

Another lesson learnt: always to walk at your own pace, even if it means walking alone. I peel and apply a Compeed plaster and start again, more carefully.

Then somewhere ahead, the distressed sound of dogs and their frantic howling. I hope Ferdie and Estevao are ok.

Eventually the dogs calm. The sun flares, and then explodes through the trees, scattering multiple strips of light across the grey tarmac. A pair of white butterflies dances in a circle before me, tracking my steps to the Loureiro viewpoint. The six-hundred-metre climb from Combarro has taken ninety minutes.

My reward, an exhilarating view over one of the *Rias Baixas* (lower rias) that slices deep inland – four broad estuaries where fresh and salt water meet. Heat-hazed far below, the Ria Pontevedra stretches south-west. I pick out a scatter of white houses strung like pearls on a necklace between the towns of Marin and Aguete, before the coast turns south and east, towards Vigo.

A large rectangular *Variante Espiritual* sign is nearby, with its '*Usted Esta Aqui*' (You are here) confirmation that I am about four kilometres from Armentiera.

Now a more gentle climb. Ten minutes later, the tarmac crumbles under my feet at a crossroad of tracks. The route veers left, to where a 'Beware of Dogs' sign hangs on a tree. Suddenly, frantic howling explodes again, stopping me in my tracks. I move gingerly forward to discover, with relief, that the dogs are corralled in what must be the local 'pound.' They seem eager to blame me, and any other passers-by, for their incarceration.

I rush past their slavering outrage. Thankfully, the fencing holds, and their fury eventually subsides. As I reach what must be the high point, it's my turn to startle a family of four wild black horses. Clattering hooves, breaking branches in the thick forest, then a return to solitude, with only an occasional rabbit loping off the track.

Underfoot, my boots kick up little clouds of dust which drift above granite glinting like a star field. Now the whisper comes, in remembered words from William Blake: 'To see the world in a grain of sand, and a Heaven in a Wild Flower.' Some of his longing – to return to innocence and notice beauty in the everyday details – fills me.

I stop for some moments under ash trees sparkling silver-grey against a milk-blue sky. In the distance, a chainsaw starts its low grumble, then high pitched whine. A tree falls. Then the faint ring of a church bell hangs in the air. 11 a.m. At my feet, a trail of ants stretches across the track, to a waymark, and its little pile of pebbles. Also known as sorrow stones, they are brought from home by pilgrims, built into delicate mini pagodas, or moved in relays from place to place along the route. I walk across, crouch and carefully make my exchange.

Each stone represents something or somebody. Perhaps a prayer for healing, or the burdens of sorrow, anxiety. Some carry their stone from home all the way to Santiago. Others deposit and lift in daily instalments of remembrance.

A voice from somewhere in the forest. A cyclist appears talking into his headset, careering downhill. I rise and follow. The yellow and blue '*Armentiera Albergue*' sign has been altered, its two-kilometre marking increased to three. This seems more realistic, as distance markers to Albergues tend towards optimism.

Half a kilometre later, the track meets the main road, and I veer right for a few hundred metres before turning left at a *Ruta do Vino* sign and a wooden *Camino Espiritual* marker. From now on, the *Ruta do Vino* signs will serve as reserve markers all the way to Vilanova, the centre of Albarino wine production.

I see no arrows, only an occasional slapdash red cross painted onto large stones. This broad track curves right for nearly another kilometre then divides. The *Variante* path runs off and left in a series of declining turns to become a narrow earthen path beside a meandering stream.

Across the stream, a man waters his vegetable patch. Outside an ancient cottage, another one scythes the grass, its fresh green scent unlocking a memory. I stop, overcome by the smell of childhood summer embankments, dizzily rolling over and over downhill, its odour wrapped around me like a blanket, leaving flecks of green ground into a white tee shirt. When all seemed possible. The man stops, wipes the sweat from his forehead, and resumes.

A donkey, tethered to a post, looks up and stares as I descend again through this secluded vale, by walls upon walls, and stone upon moss-mottled stone. Suddenly the path peters out and emerges onto the hot sticky tarmac underfoot, at Vedado de Caza. A freehand PO 1026 sign points past stone buildings, their ground floors serving as storehouses below bedrooms with casement windows and tin roofs.

Down to my left is the first glimpse of the monastery bell tower. The widening road sweeps past a giant, modern glass and concrete Pousada – gated, locked, deserted.

At a small roundabout, the yellow arrows point right – but these are directions for the Albergue, which is two hundred metres away, then down a road to the left. I follow and talk to Carmen, its *hospitalero*. She and her daughter Maria are the ones who placed the Variante signs and maintain the yellow arrows along this section of the route.

Carmen is here every day, even at Christmas if necessary. Maria helps out when she can, at weekends and holidays. The Albergue houses sixteen bunk beds, as part of a community centre. Over the winter the centre will be extended, with more beds added. She proudly tells me that last week they hosted their one thousandth pilgrim guest.[4]

I retrace my steps, past the Café-Bars A Fonte and O Comercio and into Armentiera's Monastery courtyard. The monastery dates from the first half of the twelfth century, an affiliate of the Cistercian Order, which, under Bernard of Clairvaux, played an important part in the French commitment to Spain and the Santiago Pilgrimage. However, the 1837 secularisation of church property provoked its decline into ruin.

But, in 1963 the newly formed *Amigos de Armenteira* began a rebuilding programme. By 1989, with the restoration completed, a group of Cistercian nuns arrived from the Monastery of Alloz in Navarre.

---

[4] During the winter the Albergue was modernised. It re-opened on 30th March 2017. It now provides 32 new bunk beds, a vending machine for snacks and coffee, a dining room and a small kitchen.

Today they number eight, and each night lead a vespers service, sharing reflections and praying for the pilgrims en route to Santiago.

A Moorish floral-chequered frieze surrounds the main entrance to the church. Above is a near pristine stonework circular Rosea, with its rainbow-coloured glass scattering light on a Romanesque nave with a broad transept and semi-circular apses. An elaborate Baroque altarpiece has been added, but unlike many Spanish churches or cathedrals, it has no gold.

The old cliché is that the Spanish Empire was motivated by the trinity of Gold, Glory and God – in that order – with its gold plundered from the New World. This particularly Spanish obsession led them to accumulate imported treasure that bought foreign goods instead of developing their own products.

The church, also enriched, displayed its wealth and power through increasingly elaborate cathedral architecture and lavishly furnished interiors.

However, the harvest of empire bypassed this remote mountainside. It remained immune to opulence. For the people of Armentiera's living was in stone. The décor of this church mirrors their values, with a range of painted stone saints or Mary as a holy shepherdess, unadorned by gold leaf.

I walk out and into the adjoining cloister yard, with six arches along each wing, and intricate vaulting above. The temperature is thirty degrees. I sit in the shade along the base of an arch. My back against the cool stone, I drain my water bottle and close my eyes.

Today, 30th August is the feast day of San Ero, his exotic legend woven into the monastery's history. It begins with a knight, a Don Ero, who once lived in Armenteira. He and his wife prayed fervently for a family; their prayers for children were eventually answered by a revelation that they would instead have spiritual descendants. In later life, he is said to have founded the *Santa María de Armenteira* Monastery, eventually becoming its abbot.

He then repeatedly prayed for an understanding of what heavenly bliss would feel like. One day, as he walked through the woods surrounding the monastery, the lyric beauty of a bird's song drew him to sit entranced for what seemed like a few minutes, experiencing an epiphany that brought a deep sense of peace and contentment.

As twilight approached, he walked back to the monastery, knocked on the door, but was greeted by a monk unknown to him. The monk appeared not to recognise him either and asked who he was. When he answered that he was his abbot, Ero, the monk called others who explained that Abbot Ero had disappeared into the mountains three hundred years previously.

At this point, Ero is said to have realised that his wish had been granted, with three hundred years of heavenly bliss seeming like only three minutes of birdsong.

This notion of slipping out of linear time is powerfully echoed in other sacred stories, in other Celtic connections between Ireland and Galicia. One of which is linked to Mahee Island, in County Down, close to where I live. It houses the remains of Nendrum Monastery and its legend that of St Caolan.

While cutting timber to build a church, Caolan heard a bird singing a beautiful song on a blackthorn. He listened enthralled for what he thought was one hour of deep peace. When the bird stopped singing, he returned with his wood to continue building, only to find the church complete. He questioned a stranger who tells him that the church is dedicated to St Caolan, who disappeared two hundred years earlier. As in Armenteira, they accept his tale and rejoice.[5]

---

[5] Even further back, in Ireland's *Immrama* (Sea Voyager) tales is, 'The Voyage of Bran.' Wanting to 'get away from the noise' of a festival, Bran walks outside and hears the beautiful music of the Sidhe, the inhabitants of the otherworld. An ageless figure appears

* * *

The similarities between Galician and Irish folklore remind me again of the longstanding mythic association of Galicia with Ireland, beginning with stories of the Gaels, a nomadic people who eventually settle in Iberia, and then Ireland.[6]

Many Galicians have chosen to believe these stories of connection. In their National Anthem, they sing of Galicia as the home of Breogan. To many, the similarity of names: Galicia and Gael or Iberia and Hibernia, suggest linkages between Atlantic, romantic, wayfaring, wandering peoples who exchanged not only trade but stories. Perhaps it's a wish-association, but this preference for a Celtic origin remains attractive.

---

and sings to him, urging him to voyage across the sea to a land of beauty. He gathers companions and discovers an island of joy where they live for a year. On his return, he is told that Bran set out hundreds of years earlier to seek a mystical land and has not been heard of since. Like Ero and Caolan, he had slipped out of temporal and into eternal time.

[6] The eleventh-century Irish *Book of Invasions* outlines the tale of the Gaels migration to Ireland. King Breogan, taken to be the founding father of the Galician Celtic nation, builds the city of Brigantia (associated with modern day Corunna) and constructs a giant tower. From its summit, his sons, or the sons of Miled (the Milesians) glimpse a beautiful green land in the distance and sail to conquer it. There they fight and defeat the Tuatha De Danaan (the Irish pagan-God race) who sink beneath the earth to live in the sacred mounds and barrows, and in the wells and streams. The Gaels remain to become the ancestors of the Irish people.

It also emphasises the notion of their historic nationality, their ethnic distinction from the rest of the peninsula, which may be mobilised as a resource in pursuit of either greater autonomy or independence.

Something bouncing on the cloister paving beneath me, startles me, opening my eyes. A water bottle, mine, slipped from my grasp. I must have drifted for a moment in the sultry heat. My body has stiffened, and pins and needles cramp my right leg, so I get down from the cloister arch and move haltingly, out to the courtyard.

I wonder if tonight there will be fireworks in the sky to commemorate San Ero's feast day. Or a procession like elsewhere, of a church army of clergy and villagers, their banners unfurled before the local saint, shouldered on a palanquin. Once, I heard a xylophone striking triads that hung in the air below puffs of white smoke flowering high above, followed by the Rockets delayed thunder.

I ask the barman in O Comercio if there will be any celebrations. He knows nothing about it, only vespers tonight as usual. 'They also have accommodation there, if you want to stay the night,' he says.

I thank him anyway but say that after getting lunch here, I'll probably walk on.

'Antia will take your order in a minute,' he says.

I choose a table under the bar's vine-strewn awning and sit down. There is little activity outside, just an occasional car drawing up, and a few couples coming and going in slow-step through heat pressing down like a vice. San Ero's memorial day is passing almost unnoticed, slipped from memory just as he once slipped out of time.[7]

Antia arrives, and I ask her to explain a little of the recipe, which is in Gallego. She explains that *Lentellas con Verdura* is lentils with vegetables and *Caldo Gallego* is a traditional broth made of green beans, chard, cabbage and parsnip tops.

Gallego is her first language she stresses. 'It's vital to us. Without Gallego, there is no Galicia.'

I follow her recommendation and order a lunch of *Llentellas* and fresh *Pimientos de Padron* (green peppers deep fried in olive oil and sprinkled with coarse salt).

I tell her I have been reading about Martin Sarmiento. Her eyes light up. 'Aah, yes. He is a great hero for us Galicians. He was a great lover of our language and our homeland.'

Facing the Monastery's courtyard, I sip a cold beer, then glance at some of my notes on how

---

[7] The legend was kept alive by the locally born playwright and writer, Ramón María del Valle Inclán in his 1907 work, 'Aromas de Leyenda' (Aromas of Legend), a collection of fourteen poems inspired by Galician tales, landscape, and traditions.

Sarmiento tried to serve Galicia's culture and the story of Gallego itself, its romance language, born of Latin invasion.[8]

In 1754, from Pontevedra, he made both coastal and mountainous treks west, to Vilanova, Noia and Ribiera, then north, beyond Santiago and through the La Coruna and Ferrol regions, gathering information and collecting Galician words, songs, literature.

He came to advocate that children should be taught in their own language, not Castillian, utilising many more examples from nature. When allied to the transmission of the latest scientific agricultural techniques, these innovations, he believed, would better combat illiteracy and raise living standards.

The popularity of his ideas regarding the use of Gallego ebbed and flowed until Franco again branded Gallego as backward and divisive, which, if spoken, resulted in punishment. As late as the

---

[8] Until the tenth century, both Galicians and Portuguese spoke the same tongue. Then came a split from its Latin roots, and eventual repression by Castilian authorities in the sixteenth and seventeenth centuries. Martin Sarmiento cried out against Castilian dominance, and for a diverse cultural landscape. He refused to accept the designation of Galicia by the educated and aristocratic classes as backward, inferior. Increasingly Sarmiento focused on the collection and compilation of Galician culture, geography, and language, because to him, the loss of a language or culture would be as much of a tragedy as the loss of an animal or plant species.

1970's, offending schoolchildren were put into stress positions for hours at a time.

Relief came with Franco's death in 1975 and the adoption of the new constitution in 1978. Though it confirmed Spanish as the 'official' language of the state, it also deemed other languages as 'official' in their autonomous regions and thereby able to be taught in schools.

In the 1980's Galicia increasingly identified itself with and declared itself part of the 'Celtic Fringe' nations of Western Europe: Brittany, Cornwall, Scotland, Wales, Ireland and the Isle of Man, claiming that Galicians also were an Atlantic people who looked north rather than south and east.

But even though four-fifths of it population now speaks Gallego, there has been no major campaign for independence, unlike the other historic nationalities in the Basque country and Catalonia, who have lower rates of fluency in Euskara and Catalan.

Galicia seems content with its status as an autonomous region within Spain, perhaps because they see themselves as the symbolic heart of this wider entity, the birthplace of the creation myth of Spain, with Santiago de Compostela housing the tomb of its national patron saint.

I put my notes away as Antia approaches with my steaming plates of *Llentellas* and *Pimientos de Padron*.

* * *

Just as I finish, a pilgrim couple catches my eye, walking slowly to the entrance of the monastery courtyard. They seem to hesitate for a moment, then turn towards the table beside me, remove their backpacks and slump exhausted onto the chairs.

One too many churches perhaps.

I say hello, and the woman says, 'A piece of cake, eh?'

'It was quite a climb,' I agree. She asks for directions to the Albergue.

'Enough for one day,' her husband says.

But not for me.

Chapter 5

Stone and Water

Nothing is softer or more flexible than water, yet nothing can resist it. (Lao Tzu)

After lunch, I walk through bright sunlight to the *Ruta Pedra e da Agua* sign, the Stone and Water route, seven kilometres downhill to Barrantes. Steep steps take me from one world into the cool of another, the mystic heart of this walk – a shallow glen with a tree canopy above and the Rio de Armenteira below. A granite stream, crystal clear, pouring from Mount Castrove. A chorus in the mystery play of water's circular motion. Rain falling, rising again through the mountain's dark interior to baptise the land, flowing home to the sea.

The Rio knows this place well, intimate with the ruins of thirty-three mills scattered along its banks, its memory from long before men toiled to harness its power. Now returned to freedom, it courses round rocks, splays over tipping points, then slides down irregular stairs, as if it were alive. A voice from heaven, the Bible says, is like the sound of many waters.

On the Stone and Water Route

Little surprise that our ancestors located deities in these lavish places, to be feared or revered, worshipped or placated.

In front of me, cream butterflies spiral around each other. Beside me, a blue damselfly settles on a leaf, its wings pressed back tight along its body, safe under the tree canopy from swooping predators. A rich indigo dragonfly, whirrs past – its iridescent wings turning turquoise, and then emerald. Another hovers for some seconds then flies after its partner. Years in preparation, they fly at most for two months.

In the East, they symbolise summer and autumn, prosperity, harmony – their glide across water said to represent a gaze beneath the surface of things. And one can understand how, in these numinous places, the whirr of mayfly, dragonfly wings became fairy wings.

For Native Americans, they signal wind-borne happiness, purity, in contrast with the malign myth that they are the devil's darning needles, sewing up the lips of noisy children.

A mother shouts out, 'Careful little ones,' as they hop-skip from stone to stone. But her words are lost in the white noise. Eventually, the river calms to weave like a translucent snake over dark rock and sand-coloured gravel, past trees wrapped in green velvet, cooled in the heat of the day.

Just past a lattice of spindled trees, giant millstones lie flat, absorbed in the path running past broken mill after mill, their roofs collapsed.

A couple who passed me earlier now lounge on a bench, smoking cigarettes.

'*De Donde Eres*?' he asks me. (Where are you from?) He is from Switzerland.

'It's beautiful there also,' I say. 'You are both very fortunate. How did you know about this place?'

'I am from here,' his wife says.

'We come back every year at this time,' her husband explains, 'to visit Imelda's family and walk the Stone and Water route. It's special, isn't it?'

'Yes. Words can't do it justice.'

'All Galicians come back, or long to,' Imelda says. 'The Prime Minister, Rajoy, he's from Pontevedra. He comes back every July to walk the *Ruta de Pedra de Agua.*'

'Ireland and Galicia,' I say 'have a lot in common: kindred spirits deeply attached to home, but forced into mass emigrations.'

'Yes, some of my family are in Buenos Aires,' she says. 'It's still the city with the biggest number of Galicians in it.'

Potato blight and compassion fatigue from those who could have helped changed everything in Ireland, I think but don't say.

She looks at me for a moment, and then as if she had heard my thoughts, says, 'We had times of hunger too, in the 1850's and thirty years later. My grandmother told me those stories. Starving masses arrived in Santiago to beg for food. So many left.'

Her husband rises to his feet. As if to shake off such memories, she swipes her palm across her face.

'But we have today. All this to enjoy,' he says. 'To walk the route one more time, until next year.'

I shake their hands and carry on. They walk uphill to Armenteira, where their car is parked.

A sign points to *Aldea La Brega*, where the path opens out into a glade. The heat again shudders from the ground, up and over stone figurines scattered as a remembrance of other lives past. A young woman bent low to lift her child; an older woman, shawled, stands further back in shadow; a boy in short trousers and long socks clutches his school satchel. A man prepares his bolas throw, while outside a small chapel, an angelic figure stands in classical robe and hood. The final figure, a mother with an infant in arms and a toddler at her feet, rests a tender hand on his curled hair – her expression set resolute. The heart of the village, before the villagers were scattered.

Wooden and stone footbridges cross the quietened river to where yellow arrows, painted on a vineyard wall, appear again. The PG 170 *Ruta*

Pedra de Agua turns right, its yellow-and-white-striped signage once again continuing riverside. One more kilometre to Barrantes.

At nearly 5.00 p.m. my skin is tight, reddened. Blisters have flared up, my legs ache. I need to stop. At the Barrantes roundabout is the Taberna-Hotel, *Os Castanos*. The traffic is constant but the beer cold, the staff friendly, the tortilla baguette enormous, and I have a room.

Two hours later, I walk back a few hundred metres, until the growl of traffic fades. As the heat of the day settles, I find a bench by the river and scribble some notes in an attempt to capture even part of this day.

Today's string of moments is already fading, disappearing into the ocean's swell, reduced to snapshots, or wafer-thin slices from an enchanted garden. A few words on a page, a faltering summons for a tapestry of summer into autumn, in this time of gathering stones, memories, to fashion an altar.

The dust has finally settled. The night is still. It's the same feeling of sweet melancholy at the end of each day's walk, a cumulative running down of the mind's meter, anxiety's hold loosened.

Eventually, as if in a dream, I walk back to the Taberna, where a ceiling fan stirs the thick heat, and I finally drift into deep sleep.

Chapter 6

The Rio Umia and Vilanova de Arousa

I'm half awake, half dreaming. Early morning seeps through my window set in the slanted ceiling of a garret bedroom. The whole summer ahead, eight weeks of it. The smell of fresh linen seems to hang everywhere, over family walks on switchback roads in the Glens of Antrim, over bike rides along the Lagan towpath; above sandy beaches, rock pools, and swimming out of your depth. The room floods with shafts of light.

Then another room comes into focus. Threads of sunlight drift through the shutters. They fall on a scallop shell tied tightly to a backpack. The soul returns from Elysian fields. But the taste, the excitement remains.

After a quick breakfast, I'm on my way again. Almost twenty kilometres to Vilanova. At the Barrantes bridge, the yellow and white horizontal stripes of the *Ruta do Rio Umia* (the PRG-173) replace the arrows.

The *Umia* rises northeast of here, and for sixty-three kilometres, irrigates the orchards and vineyards of the O Salnes valley before sliding into the Ria da Arousa near Combados, seven kilometres south of Vilanova.

The next five kilometres are a ramble along a riverside path to the *Puente de Santa Maria* and Ponteanearles, walking against the river's flow, by alder, ash, and willow; past lavish vineyards, where clusters of white Albarino grapes hang from vine terraces; past meadows where sparks fly upwards – the endless hunger quest of swallows.

I stop for a moment to watch them quarter the field, slicing the air back and forth in relentless, impossible arcs. Another day spent feeding on the wing. Soon they will fly south again.

But today not a breath of wind – as if warm, hazy summer were all there ever was or ever will be.

The sound of a fish rising. Its plash echoes through the still air. I turn to where a shoal of what look like brown trout circle then break the surface. Others, in line convoy upstream through silted water. Then serendipity. Somewhere, a boy shouts, 'Wheee.' Seconds later, he flies past on his bike, his bell ringing out the last hurrahs of summer freedom.

Two kilometres later, at the *Ponte de Cabanelas*, the route crosses to the left bank, with Ribadumia hidden on my right.

I stop before a field of yellow and purple wildflowers hosting the weave and flit of meadowlarks in gasps of flight.

Ahead, lines of alder twist into a guard of honour over the sun-dappled track. Then a sandbank appears along the river, the Arousa estuary close, salting the water. A fisherman answers my whispered inquiry, confirming that the fish are indeed *Troutas*.

Path beside the Rio Umia

The route returns to the right bank again, under the *Puente Santa Maria* at Pontearnelas – the final crossing, leaving the river behind. The path rises to parallel the main road with its figurines of agricultural workers.

A cobblestone bridge leads to the tiny *Capella de Santa Maria*, its interior shaded before a mahogany retablo set against the back wall like an ecclesiastical display cabinet featuring Mary and St Francis. The white altar cloth bears a spray of fading flowers. Underneath, propped upright, someone has left a votive offering, a bag of tiny iced pastries.

Two female walkers stop, seemingly also in admiration. One has an umbrella raised for shade.

I say, 'Hello. Buen Camino.' Rising sun patches adorn their backpacks.

'The Camino is becoming very popular in Japan,' she says.

I begin to muse on its resonance now reaching out to all seekers, Buddhist, Shinto, until the other says, 'It's a really cheap holiday,' smiles, and they both walk on.

Two hundred metres later, a roundabout's third exit points to Vilanova, twelve kilometres away, and at the top of the hill, a *Variante Espiritual* sign shows a further eighteen to Pontesecures (by boat), two more to Padron and twenty-six to Santiago. I'm getting closer.

I stop at Bar Casa Chica for long, sugary iced drinks from their freezer. Walking in temperatures of thirty degrees, sometimes even the coldest of water isn't enough. It just takes the edge off thirst.

Irish people are not made for this climate. I long for even a few minutes of a wrack-strewn rocky coast and cooling sea air.

I set off again on a roadside walk for a few hundred metres until the arrows signal towards the *Rio Pequeno* (small river) trickling past farmyards and vineyards. A woodpigeon easels into the air before a *Cruceiro* where a man has just completed repairs to its three-tiered base. He stands back proudly to assess his work and my admiration of the carved story of Adamic fall to incarnation, rising in relief on its column, like a junior twin to one of Ireland's high crosses.

The route weaves left and right. It climbs on paths and lanes scalded into silence, to a view back over today's walk.

The first of many *Ruta do Vino Rias Baixas* signs signal the beginnings of a long descent. Beyond the PO 549 road bridge is the first sight of the Ria Arousa, four kilometres away, on a gentle decline through the suburbs of San Roque. But it feels like an incline, my legs increasingly leaden, dragged in slow motion through the dense steamy air, my back soaked with sweat, my pack filling with wet sand.

Finally, just south of Vilanova, a glinting Caribbean view between lines of slanted fir trees. In the west, a rib of cloud rises above the horizon, the only break in the blue. Two dinghies moored to rock, their lines draped with exhausted seaweed. At the water line, a mother and son stand to face each other in gentle discussion. Their voices echo through the humid air above the water's lap, its final glisten over white sand.

In the bay, only a speedboat moves, right to left, its scar a foaming white. As if stolen from the Florida Keys, the *Punta do Castelete* road bridge curves two kilometres west, across to the *Isla de Arousa*. Beyond, on the other shore the towns of Rianxo, Boiro, A Pobra, and Ribeira – the route of another Sarmiento circuit. An Atlantic circuit.

An irresistible impulse. I shed my boots and socks, pick my way across a rocky outcrop, lie flat on my back and, scattering dozens of translucent minnows, dangle feet and ankles in gloriously cool water.

I burrow my toes into the sand. My eyes close, lulled by the water's gentle rocking. From along the beach come sunbathed children's voices. Then other voices drift in, a soundtrack from even further away, a memory glimpse of parents, aunts and uncles escaped from silent grainy celluloid, from flickering small screen premieres. The disappeared from time, gambolling again in their floral-patterned dresses, their shirt sleeves and turned-up trousers. Some, camera shy, are never ready for their close up. Others act up, cheesing out gurning grins, kicking through the waves of Monterey come to the Antrim Coast. When Camelot still shimmered.

I hold my breath a moment longer, bathed in their laughter, until the reel unravels and they fade again to silence.

I blink open my eyes to gaze across a technicolour print of luminous water merging into coast then sky, an extravagant collage burnt onto and beyond the retina, a landscape becoming a place in the heart.

In Portugal, I remember a pilgrim saying, 'At the end of the day all we're doing is walking each other home.' And I know that that's what Galicia is like – a coming home. I remember again, Columba's advice to his own wanderers, 'Let your feet follow your heart until you find the place of your resurrection.' The place where the loss adjustors of the soul deliver some repayment; where anxiety is shed like skin before a field full of treasure, the one you'd sell all you have to possess.

I sit awhile, then lace my boots up and carry my unlocked memories on the final forty minutes' walk along Terron beach; past bars and awnings that flap in an occasional breeze; past huge fir trees shadowing the water green – to the *Punto Arinho*, the white footbridge to Vilanova's town centre.

The arrows point right for the Albergue, tracking the bay along the *Rua Porto do Cabo*, to the *Avenida do Rocheo*, where a man sits flushed, perspiring in a tank top, shorts and flip-flops outside a large modern concrete and glass building. I look about for the Albergue, where I'm to meet Alfonso at five p.m.

As I turn, thinking I've walked past it, the man shouts out in a thick Dublin accent and points. 'It's in here. Upstairs.' It's a sports centre, the *Pavillion de Deportes*, part of the first floor given over to an Albergue, with gym equipment nearby should anyone feel the need to warm down after a day's walking.

I feed the drinks machine. It clunks out a bottle of water. I down it in one draught and walk upstairs to talk to the hospitalero, Emilio, telling him I'm waiting here for Alfonso. His eyes light up in recognition. I ask him how long the Albergue in Vilanova has been open.

'For three years now,' he says. 'Since the route began.'

The Albergue has fourteen bunk beds plus extra mattresses that can be set out in another room as needed.

Just then, as I take a seat to wait, someone with tousled hair, trimmed goatee and a wide-smiling welcome walks over to me.

'Roy?' he asks.

Alfonso.

Alfonso and Debee Cherene, my hosts in Vilanova de Arousa

It's a short drive to Debee and Alfonso's house in San Roque. I see their residential annexe, divided into two bedrooms, with a bathroom in between. Each room has three single beds, and thankfully no bunks. I make my selection then follow him into the house and meet Debee, who tells me I can use the kitchen anytime. 'Make a coffee or a snack. Use the living room to relax, read.'

They usher me into a room with a long table that could easily seat a dozen people.

'We have our meals in here,' Alfonso says. Something wonderful is simmering in garlic and herbs. 'Seven o' clock, for dinner?'

I nod my head enthusiastically, suddenly aware that I'm now more hungry than thirsty.

After a shower, I relax on the veranda overlooking their garden framed by laurel and walnut trees. A wood pigeon settles in a beech tree, cooing out its reassurance. A swing roped beneath a bough, and towels hung from a line, are both motionless as the temperature rises this last day of August, a dog day of summer torpor.

I phone my wife and tell her that most of my walking is over, as I plan to stay here tomorrow and explore.

Thirty minutes later, Alfonso calls me inside, to a mouth-watering dish of garlic chicken and rice, salad and a smooth home-made Albarino wine gifted by a friend.

'The neighbours are generous here,' he says. 'They keep giving us vegetables, fish, as well as wine!'

After dinner, they explain a little of their journey.

Alfonso is originally from Brazil and Debee from Guernsey. In 1980, while they were both working in Madrid, they met and subsequently married.

They lived in the Madrid area for over thirty-five years, but for a long time thought about moving north, to the Camino.

'Eventually, just a few months ago we found this place to rent,' Alfonso says. 'We wanted to open up a house for pilgrims, to provide them with a service, in a family environment on a *donativo* (donation) basis. Not in competition with the Albergues but in addition to them.'

'In most Albergues, pilgrims can only stay for the one night. Right?' I ask.

'Yes, in most cases,' Debee says. 'But here, pilgrims can stay for more than one night – if they need time to process all that has happened to them on the walk. A lot of emotions can rise to the surface. Sometimes people need a place where they can relax, talk things through, and if they wanted, we could pray with them.'

'And this new route is exciting,' Alfonso says. 'On the Variante, everything isn't developed yet, like the other routes. I think it attracts a different type of pilgrim, someone who doesn't expect things to be easy, someone who ...wants to see something new. Someone with ... how do you say...?'

He turns to Debee and says something in Spanish.

' A different mentality?' Debee asks.

'Yes. A different mentality. Often they are people walking on their own. There are few large groups here as yet.'

'Our son Dani worked here over the summer,' Debee says, 'sometimes as an interpreter on the boat and other times as a volunteer in the Armenteira Albergue.'

She tells me he was captivated by the beauty of the section after Armenteira, the Stone and Water route, so much that he walked it back and forth three times.

It strikes me that more such places as this are needed, with people of faith, like Alfonso and Debee.

'It's good to have an opportunity to process things before you finish the walk,' I tell them, 'because sometimes there can be a feeling of anti-climax. And if the high point is presented as the Pilgrim Mass – in a language that many don't understand – that that can be a problem, because the next day, most of us are on a plane home.'

There few understand the depth of the Camino experience and even fewer understand its emotional resonance.

'Yes, more places like this are needed,' I say. 'Many of us have to work it through on our own, trying to grapple with the depth of our attraction to this phenomenon. For, of course, the Camino doesn't end with Santiago.'

'Yes,' Alfonso says. 'The most important thing is what you do when you get back, how you integrate those feelings into your life.'

I show them a few pictures from my Camino Frances, some of an Albergue in Carrion de Los Condes, run by nuns.

'You stayed with the Little Sisters in Carrion,' Alfonso says. 'I met some of them last year, in Avila, where their home monastery is. They have a service each night for the pilgrims. It's very moving.'

I tell them about my night in Carrion, in the Santa Maria Albergue, where the sisters prepared a small crayoned paper star for each of us.

'Why a paper star?' Debee asks.

'Because love is light,' they said. 'Like paper,' and, 'light for the way, bringing hope for the future.'

That night, the spiritual journey was approached sensitively – in the context of a pilgrimage no longer reduced to metaphor.

I say, 'I remember, at home, reading someone who argued against the need for pilgrimage by saying that God is the same everywhere. He may be, I thought, but I'm not.'

Alfonso nods. 'That's important. People from

many traditions are rediscovering the importance of meditation, and the practice of pilgrimage. We need an ecumenical approach to supporting pilgrims.'

'That's something we love,' Debee adds, 'bridge-building between our differing traditions.'

It seems to me they represent a new network rising to serve from all denominations.

I want to learn more, but after another long day's walk, I begin to flag, make my apologies and head to bed. Tomorrow will be a day for exploring Vilanova, with Alfonso as my guide.

Chapter 7

Exploring Vilanova and the Isla de Arousa

After breakfast, we drive down alongside the Ria de Arousa, its water glistening at the start of the day. It seems idyllic, but I know it hasn't always been that way.

In the 1980's, most of the Colombian cocaine that came into Europe arrived on this coastline, via the *planeadoros*, the fast boats. But when local teenagers began to get hooked on cocaine, a group of mothers from Vigo turned on the drug lords and started a campaign. Arrests were made, and properties confiscated, turned into community centres.

Now fishing seems the biggest industry. In Galicia, it employs over 400,000 people.

'Tonnes of seafood are harvested here in the *Rias Biaxis* (the lower Rias),' Alfonso says, 'with the *Arousa* the largest ria.'

As we drive along the bay, he points towards a mass of rafts (*bateas*). 'There are 2,700 of them out there. Underneath each are huge chains of mussels growing on ropes.'

I say the seafood here is the best I've ever tasted. 'Why is it so good?'

'They say it's the mix of salt and fresh water, full of all the silt washed off the land. From here it's delivered all over Spain and abroad.'

I later read that they are the second highest exporter of mussels in the world.

We drive out of town for a few kilometres and up to a viewpoint – once the location of the medieval Castelo de Lobeira, nestled between giant granite boulders. The hilltop was both the site of a castro (circular settlement) from the Celtiberian period (the first millennia BC), and the birthplace of Teodomiro, the ninth century Bishop of Iria Flavia to whom the hermit Pelayo relayed his tale of stars falling on a remote hillside. Teodomiro rushed to excavate the site, found three skeletons, and in 813 AD declared it the tomb of St James and his faithful disciples, Teodoro and Anastasius.

The castle, also erected in the ninth century, was reinforced to defend against Viking, Norman, and Mulsim attacks. Its strategic position overlooking the *Ria Arousa* offered, along with the *Torres Oeste* (West Towers) at Catoria, a forward defence system for Santiago known as 'The Doors to Compostela.' The castle's ownership was transferred to the Archbishopric of Santiago until finally razed in a fifteenth-century anti-feudal popular revolt. More recently, it was again a battleground, with Civil War Republican units and refugees bombed on the summit.

But today it is deserted as I climb through furnace heat past granite boulders. On the summit, above a holm oak, stands an even greater rock, its angles like the prow of a ship, topped by a guard rail and simple wooden cross. Bolted to its keel, a metal plate erected by the British Admiralty memorialises the 173 officers and men from HMS Serpent, lost on 10th November 1890, north of here, close to *Cabo Vilan* and Camerinas on the infamous *Costa Del Morte* (Coast of Death).

The Serpent, with its crew of apprentice sailors, had set sail from Plymouth for the Cape of Good Hope only two days earlier. But off Camerinas heavy seas drove them onto rocks six hundred metres offshore. The ship sank in less than an hour, one of the deadliest shipwrecks off the coast of Galicia. Local people still hold a ceremony of remembrance every year. The sense of tragedy heightened by the victims' youth perhaps serves as a cypher for all the region's losses at sea.

* * *

Our next stop is the *Isla de Arousa*, where the *Punta do Castelete* road bridge stretches two kilometres to a resort island with biking trails, boardwalk beaches of coarse yellow sand, and busy restaurant-bars. Its southern shores host a nature reserve and on its far side a lighthouse.

'Xufre, the main town, is to the north,' Alfonso says, pointing, 'with two small ports. That is where the *Arousana*, the seafood festival, is held in early August.'

We drive past the *O Con do Forno* viewpoint and to the nineteenth-century lighthouse, sited on a group of giant rocks, and now recommissioned as a restaurant. I walk along its wooden decking, past a scattering of families sipping soft drinks, or white wines, overlooking the small beach of *Faro de Punta del Caballo* (the lighthouse at the tip of the horse). The map of the Isla resembles the outline of a pony, now tethered to the land by the bridge.

I turn for a moment and gaze across to the Barbanza Peninsula and the fishing towns of O Pobra and Ribeira, wondering what this setting would be like at sunset – the same coastline to which Sarmiento inquisitively peered across in 1745.[1]

---

[1] He spent most of the final twenty years of his life in Madrid, devoted to research. Sarmiento died on 7th December 1772, with few of his works published or proposals implemented. Rather, his ideas were committed to a long gestation before bearing fruit in the late twentieth-century, along with his belated recognition as the first apostle of Galician culture – someone far ahead of his time. In 1994, the Padre Sarmiento Institute of Galician Studies was established in Santiago in his honour.

Standing in the sunlight glittering on diamond water, I'm reminded of why he loved being in the open air, studying nature, wandering around this coast. For him, as for Irish Celtic Christians, nature was another living, sacred text that required careful examination. He surely knew of, and closely followed St Columbanus's advice that 'If you want to know the creator, you must first understand his creation.'

Just as many early monastic giants exhibited an almost pagan veneration for nature, perhaps in our post-Christian world, this sense of reconnection with nature, enabled by the Camino experience, may signpost many of us back to wonder, and belief.

It's late afternoon, and I have to cut short my reverie.

As we drive back across the bridge, I ask Alfonso, 'Who came up with the proposal to add the Spiritual Variant to the Camino Portuguese?'

'It came from Celestino Lores, the president of the Federation of Amigos del Camino Portuguese.'

He explains that after discussions with local civic leaders, they jointly submitted their proposal to the Santiago Cathedral authorities who approved this new route in 2013. 'It was the cathedral authorities who named it the *Variante Espiritual*, in acknowledgement of the impact of Padre Sarmiento and the monasteries of Poio and Armentiera.'

Alfonso goes on to tell me that in June the local *Concellos* (Councils) launched a separate but complimentary Sarmiento trail, the *Ruta Padre Sarmiento*, a coastal route starting in Poio. It winds west and north through Combarro, Sanxenxo, Portonovo, O Grove, Cambados, Vilanova, the Isla de Arousa, Villagarcia and finally Padron, to link with the Camino Portuguese.

'Next year my wife and I will return,' I tell him, 'explore that route and spend more time here.'

'Yes, you should,' he says, 'then we will put two beds together for you.'

* * *

Later that evening Thomas rings to see how I was getting on. Now in Santiago, he plans to spend a couple of days in Muxia. 'So I can see somewhere new,' he says.

I tell him I will be in Santiago on Saturday and will see him there.

* * *

Over a dinner of lamb couscous, Alfonso confirms that the departure time of tomorrow morning's boat to Padron as 7.30, in virtual darkness. I'd see nothing. So, I have to decide if I should stay an extra night in Vilanova and hope for a later departure, the next day. This meant that I might not have time to walk the final twenty kilometres to Santiago. I didn't like that, even though I had walked it in 2012.

I step out into the velvety darkness, and stare up at the Milky Way, sixteen hundred light years distant, and listen to the trees sing their cicada songs of summer.

I remind myself that this trip was not about gaining a Compostela or covering every kilometre but, rather, intentionally walking slower and taking the time to explore. So I decide to stay, and tomorrow check the walking option towards Padron. I hope it may have some sections along the water's edge that give closer views of the seventeen Crucerios that line the sea road, the Via Maritima.

Chapter 8

Walking Again – Carill, Catoria and Padron

I sleep well, until dawn breaks, to cockerel cries at seven a.m. Bleary eyed, I wander into the garden. A white vapour coats the land. The air is crisp, fresh. Seville marmalade, thick-cut toast and strong coffee buoy me up for another walk on a scalding September day.

Alfonso leaves me to the town centre, close to the Albergue, from where I begin my walk back around the bay, past the footbridge and the Porto de Vilanova, along the Prias da Sinas and out onto the main road, the PO 548.

At café bar Esmeralda I turn left down the Rua Viega do Mar for a waterside walk past the cranes of Vilagarcia docks.

The Sarmiento Route signs and the Spiritual Variant arrows take me along a kilometre of Compostela Beach to the fishing port of Carill – a two-hour walk of just over nine kilometres.

I stop outside a café and order an Americano. Just opposite, offshore, lies the island of Cortegada, the verdant *La Isla de Los Laureles*, where the Rio Ulla's fresh water meets the salt of the Arousa estuary.

At low tide, a causeway is revealed, built on a sandbar and known locally as 'the road of the cart.' Here, the tides change quickly. It's a treacherous crossing, but one now rarely made, as Cortegada has lain uninhabited for over a century. Today, it's a nature reserve, part of the Galician National Parks.

The island appears almost rectangular. It's 130 acres covered in dense woodland, which includes the largest remaining forest of bay laurel in Europe, a dramatic reversal from a time when laurel covered much of the Mediterranean basin. Before Cortegada became a ghost island, its monks once propagated as many as 300 varieties of laurel.

The trees hide uncultivated meadows. Only crumbled dwellings, and the remains of a seventeenth-century monastery, church, pilgrim hospital and leper house stand in silent witness to activity long past.

Collared doves, then wood pigeons burst from the trees. On the shoreline a scatter of cormorants settle into a motionless pose, staring out over the ria, their wings transfigured to dry in the morning breeze.

I close my eyes for a moment, and in my imagination, the forest smells of laurel and shellfish

– the aroma of clams, cockles, razors and bay leaves stirred together.

I open my eyes, finish my coffee, and type Cortegada into my phone's search bar.

One site explains that the island now has a visitors' reception centre and two circular routes: a complete circuit and one across the middle through laurel and eucalyptus. Some local companies offer transport and guided routes.

I get up and resume my walk, following the PO 548 for another kilometre along the coast. It then turns inland to a major roundabout with its third exit (left and north) pointing to Catoria, eight kilometres away along a dangerous main road.

Just past the cemetery, I cross a bridge over the railway line and try to cut down to the water's edge, but a gardener tells me there is no way through until 'after a large rock at the next overpass.'

I retrace my steps out onto the main road, until, just past Bamio campsite, I try again, cutting left down a small road running parallel with the Carretera. I pick up an earthen track which takes me to the first of seventeen crosses erected in the 1960s to promote the final stages of James's sea route.

I carefully pick my way through brambles, then over a wrack-strewn low- tide shoreline. Above, the hunting cries of a pair of kestrels. I disturb a stork, also intent on its prey. It shrieks an angry cry and takes a flight up and over the cross, four metres high, with an image of Christ facing the Ria Arousa. Attached half way down the stone column is a weathered statuette of what must be James. In a place usually inaccessible, I sit a while in the morning breeze as fishing boats drift past under a cloudless sky.

I'm glad I did as this was the only Crucerio accessible. Four more attempts met thick bushes, brambles, with only the distant view of a triad of crosses, representing James and his disciples, Teodoro and Anastasias.

By the time I reach Catoria, I know that the boat is the better option. I decide instead to explore Catoria's twin West Towers.

A walkway snakes out to the *Torres Oeste*, an adjoining capela and the remains of a walled compound, defence against Viking, Norman, and Muslim raiders. On one side of each tower, gap-toothed crenelles remain, from which defenders loosed arrows on the attackers below.

The remains of the towers now look more like thrones for a pair of decommissioned Titans, tasked to oversee family picnics and excited children clambering over the rocks. Two garish red and blue replica Viking longboats lie anchored off shore, a reminder from early August when a procession of boats sails along the Arousa estuary and the Rio Ulla commemorating the Translatio.

I sit by the water's edge. Tomorrow morning my boat will pass by, and I remember how often, in mythic journeys, water brings the wanderer home. Now new generations of wanderers criss-cross Europe, some on journeys of meaning, others on flights for physical survival.

On a previous Camino, I talked with Martin, a Boston priest on sabbatical. I asked him, 'Do you think we're just indulging ourselves here, while all over the Mediterranean, people are strapping on life jackets and climbing into boats? Should we not be addressing *that* instead of walking this path?'

He took a moment before answering. 'But we can choose to do something about that when we get back. Do you not think that being here, even for a while, is important? Are *we* not also in need of help, of setting things straight?'

'Sometimes,' I said, 'it feels as if there's a hole in the centre of this world, and everything good is draining away, falling through it: Syria, Iraq.'

He nodded, then said, 'Perhaps, in some small way we're laying strands of a net that might catch some of the values we've let slip. And what we experience here of real community might help us to offer that in the future.'

* * *

His words echo with me today, as I sit and stare at the water's flow. Then a text arrives. I look away and read Alfonso's message. He's picked up a ticket from the Albergue, for tomorrow's boat, confirming a departure time of eight a.m. The journey will not be in darkness.

Then he sends me a poster message of calm waters in the morning sun, looking like a view from the *Isla de Arousa*. Its caption: 'You can't do anything about the length of your life, but you can do something about its width and depth.'

I get up, stretch stiff limbs and walk back to Catoria, as there is one more place where I want to spend time today. I take the train north to Padron, and Mount Santiaguino, a site that few visit, but according to legend, the place where James preached his first sermon in Spain.

* * *

As the carriage doors close, I sit and read some of my notes on the Translatio. The twelfth-century *Codex Calixtinus*, the *Liber St Jacobi* recounts that, after James's beheading in AD 44, his body was taken from Jerusalem to Jaffa by Teodoro and Anastasias and placed aboard a stone boat. In a miraculous week, it was angel-propelled across the Mediterranean, then north along the Galician coast to land just outside what was then the Roman city of Iria Flavia.

For he had been here before. Tradition claims the Padron area as the starting point of St James's missionary work in Spain, his heartland, resonant with his myth.

After Teodoro and Anastasias had tied their bowline to a large stone stele at a hamlet outside Iria Flavia, they turned first to the local Queen Lupa (the Wolf Queen) for help in finding a suitable place to bury the Apostle. Initially, she appeared helpful, but her advice was malign. Perhaps conscious of a threat to her pagan belief system, she sent them to Regulus, the Roman governor of Dugium, near Finisterre, with assurances that he would grant them the necessary land.

But Regulus was also the high priest of the pagan cult Ara Solis, and instead of assisting, he imprisoned them. However, that night, in response to prayer, their cell door opened and they escaped, returned to Lupa and renewed their request.

She then sent them to a 'Sacred Peak' North-East of Iria Flavia. There, she assured them, beneath its forested slopes they would find oxen that could be yoked to the cart carrying James and transport them to a place of their choice. However, the supposedly docile oxen turned out to be wild bulls. But the sign of the cross reduced them to quiescence, and they were harnessed to the cart. A giant snake (or dragon) then threatened. This time the cross dispatched it. When the disciples returned (again) to Queen Lupa, with the now tame bulls pulling the bier, she converted to Christianity.

The disciples now determined to let the bulls choose the Apostle's final resting place. They stop a few miles later beneath Mount Libredon, and James is laid to rest. Then, somehow, the site lay forgotten for 600 years.

* * *

A few kilometres before Padron, I put my notebook away to gaze at the lavish green. Then cottage gardens full of wild roses race past my window. The train slows, the doors hiss open and steamy air rushes in.

I walk from the station, past Rosalio Castro's former home now a museum to her memory, and towards a densely wooded hillside familiar to her, a place of 'hoary holm-oak groves … where silence extends her wings.'[1]

I stop at the Tourist Office on the Avenida de Compostela to collect any leaflets on Monte Santiaguino.

'It's mentioned briefly in these, I think,' the tourist officer says.

---

[1] From her 1884 poem, 'On the banks of the Sar'

'How old is the shrine?'

'2,000 years old,' he says.

I look at him, surprised.

He continues. 'The legend says that the Apostle James preached there … if you believe that.' Just the hint of a smile appears.

'How old is the statue set there?' I ask.

'As old as the chapel. From the fifteenth or sixteenth century. But before that, the site was, how you say? A pagan place, at least 3,000 years old.'

'A Celtic high place,' I say. 'Then Christianised, claimed by the church?'

'Yes, most likely.'

'It's strange that the statue only dates from the sixteenth century when pilgrimage numbers were falling away.'

'Perhaps it was an attempt to revive interest,' he says.

'That would make sense, but he's not dressed there as James Pilgrim or Matamoros (the Moorslayer) but as a first-century Aramean.'

'Yes indeed. Most unusual.' He smiles. 'A mystery, one might say.'

Chapter 9

Mount Santiaguino

I walk back along the Rio Sar, through the tunnel of giant plane trees, past the statue of Rosalia Castro and the Church of St James. It houses the *Pedron*, the mooring post dedicated, 'To Neptune. From the Forum of Iria Flavia.'

Across the medieval bridge is the sixteenth-century fountain, the *Fonte do Carme*. Above its arch, a relief of the arrival and mooring of James' water-borne coffin. Then higher still, in a niched recess, a representation of James personally baptising a repentant Queen Lupa.

Fifty metres to the right of the Fonte, a sign points to the *Escaleras Santiaguino*, the stairs of St James, framed by twin pillars, one with the Santiago sword symbol, the other featuring a large shell motif, crossed by pilgrim staves and gourds.

The steps ascend the hillside in blocks of five until moss-covered walls rise on both sides of the laneway. Dappled sunlight flares through chestnut trees onto stones smoothed by centuries of footfall.

The lane ends a hundred metres later. To my left, the first sight of the chapel, originally a hermitage, then the tomb of a fifteenth-century canon. Jacobean tradition claims the Apostle James preached here, and then, like Moses, struck a stone with his staff, from which water miraculously flowed. Steps descend to where the font continues to pour out through the rock on which they built a church.

Above the spring is another relief of a pilgrim James baptising an enraptured Lupa. A focus on the conversion of pagan royalty was a common strategy, deployed by Patrick, Columba, Aiden and Cuthbert as well as the deceased James. Legends surrounding their arrivals to preach the gospel all record power encounters with local pagan rulers, as kingdoms clashed in the early centuries AD.

Across the green is another enclosure, the place I've returned to visit. Above a flat foundation rock, enormous weather-beaten granite boulders have been levered into place, stone wedged against stone. They cradle what looks like a Celtic high altar long before it became a Jacobean shrine.

Above six full steps, a miniature James no more than four feet tall stands on a plinth in the midst, clothed in first-century robes. His right hand is raised to clutch a fold in his garment as if he's about to address the senate. An empty cross rises behind and above him. No transfigured Christ in freeze-framed agony and no Mary at his back.

Instead, it resonates with an earlier scene, a sermon on another mount – in a setting where a simple, naïve statue of a full-bearded Galilean mimics the behaviour of his cousin become Messiah. In his hand, the remains of what looks like a club that actually could break open a rock.

Mount Santiguinio, Padron

Alone in the silence between birdsong, I lie back on the coarse grass. It prickles through my shirt and on my arms. Scattered amongst the mix of pine, holm oak and plane trees are six Edwardian lampposts.

An echo of a Narnian wood between the worlds, in this Celtic 'thin place'. The membrane between the material and the spiritual world made porous by prayer.

The Wood between the Worlds – Mount Santiaguino

And I think again of the myth, the trope that got us walking, and the works of Joseph Campbell and C.S. Lewis, suggesting that myth charts the story of mankind's spiritual quest.

Though Lewis acknowledged paganism's profound insight, that all of the creation is sacred, alive and deeply connected, he claimed that Christianity *fulfilled* paganism. For him, the myths (without root in historical facts) were mere waymarks awaiting the arrival of what he called 'The one true myth.' The stories of dying and rising gods, he argued, were fulfilled through the incarnation, death, and resurrection of Christ. The Christian story was, therefore, unique. It was the moment when 'Myth Became Fact'.[1]

But then, in the place in between promise and fulfilment, we reverted to our default setting and carried on regardless, with the church now weaving elaborate new myths around historical figures such as James.

Despite this, the Camino has now taken on a life of its own, uncoupled from the legend. The positive effects are many.

It has sparked a return to deeply humane primal basics, the Camino modelling out the core principles of early Celtic Christianity: the shedding of home comforts to live more simply; a dependence on the hospitality of others; a reconnection with nature, ourselves and the Other, through the practice of pilgrimage. Its voice, one

---

[1] Lewis in World Dominion, Oct 1944, 270.

from long before our divisions, offering solid common ground for all Christian traditions.

Again, as with my last visit, four years ago, a serene atmosphere hovers. It's as if this place speaks to some ancient shared memory, of sermons actually preached here, if not by James, then later, by hermits, canons, bishops. Something is echoing to this ever faithful congregation of flowing water and silent stone under wind-rushed trees; to sparrows, doves, and today, me; something of Julian of Norwich's mystical insight, of God 'as the only Verb, the single action that moves through every human and earthly deed.'

Just as the evergreen holm oak, stubborn and resistant to drought, remains, so also the hope bound up within the James myth, again reaches out to redefine so many lives into two states: a new BC and AD – before and after their Camino.

Tomorrow I will be in Santiago Cathedral, a highlight of medieval architecture, intended as a tribute to divinity, contrived to provoke wonder. But today the wonder is here, where the oak tree roots tunnel deep and wide, a forest church under the vast vault of sky, worth every sweated step from somewhere East of Eden.

Scientists have discovered that even in stone, water is buried deep within. Even in stony hearts it occasionally comes to the surface. My vision blurs.

In the silence a conversation between stone and water, at almost the end of this journey.

Then the sound of the wind above, like a waterfall through the trees. A branch breaking somewhere. An echoed snap and fall. I remember San Ero and check my watch. I have only been here for an hour. It seems longer. I rise to leave but stop twice to look back, then turn a walled corner, and descend the 125 steps to return to Vilanova.

* * *

After dinner, I sit awhile in Alfonso and Debee's garden, the air still, like the rest between breaths. Then I wander down and stand under one of their laurel trees. Its leaves leathery, their surface a burnished dark green. I tear one open, releasing its sweet aroma.

In the games of ancient Greece, dedicated to Apollo, wreaths of *Laurus Nobilis* (the noble laurel) were woven together into a crown and presented as a symbol of victory and honour. Hence, one could then 'rest on one's laurels.' The Christian church came to associate laurel with martyrdom, with those who 'persevere under trial,' receiving the 'victor's crown of eternal life' promised to those who love God.[2]

---

[2] See James 1:12, 2 Tim 2:5.

The brothers James and John, in response to their request for high positions in His coming kingdom, were assured by Jesus only of a share in his sufferings. I think of the path he walked, the crown he gained, and remember that for everything there is indeed a season.

Like the damselfly after a long gestation, James has also reemerged iridescent, after *his* long hibernation; his colour changing in the eye of each beholder, to accommodate a range of meaning. His wounds again the place where the light enters; his spilt blood the seed for countless journeys of delayed appreciation.

As the sun sets over the Barboza Peninsula, and as the light sluices away, the lamps of O Pobra begin to shimmer through the evening air. A soft wind blows – a summer zephyr, a west wind gently stirring the leaves.

So many of us blown to Galicia by a desert wind, an easterly Scirroco. Until, the vane changes, returning us with a new trove of moments, become as light as a paper star, soaring high in the air of home. The myth of James, now translated into millions of lives, his story become ours.

Chapter 10

Translatio

As I leave Alfonso and Debee's house, the air is morning-fresh, pine-scented, the purple bougainvillaea cascading from below shuttered windows, framing their door. I will miss this place and their kindness.

Alfonso leaves me down to the pier, the boat just entering the harbour; an inflatable, high powered launch with seating for eight, its sailing times tide dependent. If the numbers of pilgrims increase, he tells me, they will put on a second trip each day.

I am the first to arrive, then another pilgrim, Laura from Valencia. She started walking in Coimbra.

'How was it?' I ask her.

'Very very hot.' she says.

I say my goodbyes, pass across my rucksack and step into the boat.

Then Emilio from the Albergue ushers five more pilgrims forward, Spanish, French and English. As they board in the morning mist, the captain jauntily tells us that his name is Santiago. 'And that is where we are going.' I note that the lifejackets remain underneath the seats. As we reverse from the harbour and into open water, the sun is yet to rise behind Vilanova.

Me about to board the boat for the Translatio route to Pontesecures

But, within a few minutes, it's as if someone lights a beacon behind the blue-grey hills. It flares upwards, pouring out yellow streamers from a smelted sun that ripple in fiery traces across the surface of the bay. Ahead are the mussel farm's dark rafts.

Santiago opens the throttle, pushing our bodies backwards as we navigate a sea road into open water. Passing Cortegada Island, I see traces of the stone dock and a glimpse of crumbling cottages.

Laura and I are in the prow of the boat. As ice-cold air rushes over us, we unpack ponchos and wrap them around our legs. Those behind zip their jackets high or raise bandanas over their mouths, to look like pirates skimming across the Ria.

We disturb a stork. 'It's a good omen,' Laura says. It flies low, each beat of its wingtips almost sweeps the water. The sun like a searchlight across the bay catches a cormorant in its flare, while on our left, hills loom like banks of dark cloud above a land still misted white.

Water laps the base of our first Cruceiro, the one I clambered to yesterday, again surrounded. Then a trinity of crosses appears on a larger island, with Christ high and central. Just past the island is a dense pine wood set in rows. Deep in the darkening tunnels between, the mist drifts to create ghost shapes, a fitting audience for a ghost journey, for Translatio, the transfer of the remains of James.

We pass the pine woods with their Celtic mists, then through the stanchions of Catoria's high-speed railway bridge, where a silver train arrows across to Santiago, the sun glinting on its windows. More crosses, but far away. Then the *Torres de Oeste*, the still impressive 'Doors to Santiago.'

The estuary narrows to become the Rio Ulla. We glide over calm water, and past reed banks, where scimitar-shaped swifts swoop from the sky as larks rise. A cloud pillar of steam rises from a lumber mill as we approach Pontesecures, our journey ending before an industrial wharf.[1]

After an hour in the rush of cold air, with numbed hands we hoist packs, ready to walk, shivering, onto the pier.

The pilot says, 'Two days ago, the sailing time was at 2.30 p.m.'

That would have been a very different trip, in the thirty-degree heat on a humid afternoon.

'But we have no control of the tides,' he explains.

The sailings times differ each day. Yesterday, at 7.30 a.m. we would have seen little in the half-light.

We pick up the first arrows on our left and stretch out in ones and twos, become once again a straggled line of morning pilgrims, with the Rio Sar on our left for the final kilometres to Padron.

I walk with Henry from London. I tell him a little about Mount Santiaguino ahead, of its Edwardian lampposts, its C. S. Lewis ambience of a wood between the worlds.

'Aah, Narnia,' he says. ' I read the *Chronicles* to my daughter when she was young. It was our evening ritual.'

---

[1] Pontesecures means the bridge of Caesar. A first-century Roman bridge was erected in this town said to remind Emperor Augustus of his childhood home.

My mind now races, sifting out evidence of any other connections between Lewis, pilgrimage and Ireland.

Though Lewis didn't walk the Camino, I now realise he not only represented the symbols of pilgrimage in the memorial window (including the galleon) but also some of its themes in the imagined *Voyage of the Dawn Treader*.

Might this tale be rooted in Irish folklore, in the *Immrama* tales of Christian or Pagan voyagers such as Bran or St Brendan the Navigator, on heroic sea journeys to the Otherworld, located somewhere far to the west? Perhaps Lewis takes this template, only to reverse it, with the destination now the Utter East of Aslan's kingdom, the east from which Christ will also return.

And on this pilgrim-type voyage, the characters are confronted with their flaws.

The boy Eustace, infected by avarice, turns into a dragon. But he is led to a well by Aslan, where layers of scaly skin are peeled off. He then bathes in a pool of healing water, restored in new clothes to both humanity *and* innocence.

The imagery seems to allude to a central trope of pilgrimage: that of shedding skins, possessions, worries and desires; the scene reminiscent of the pilgrim practice of washing in the waters off Finisterre, symbolically scrubbing off the old skin, in a ritual of death and rebirth.

Then to finally compound the Irish connection, Reepicheep, the valiant mouse boards a coracle to complete his pilgrim journey, up and over the wall of water, the final barrier to Aslan's Kingdom.

On an even wider canvas, might it be possible that the Irish *Immrama* stories influenced the legend of James and his return? Were they also traded back to Galicia?

The fact that both pagan and Christian *Immrama* tales were written down by Irish monks from the eighth century onwards lends some weight to this. Could these stories have passed along the church's monastic communications network, just as elements of folklore were earlier exchanged back and forth between Galicia and Ireland?

My thoughts are interrupted by Henry saying something.

'Sorry?' I say, then apologise. 'I was somewhere else.'

'Can you give me the directions to Mount Santiaguino? I have never heard of it before.'

'Of course.'

The approaches are quiet, as the first heat of the sun starts to defrost stiff limbs. We walk past Saturday market traders erecting their stalls, and linger over morning coffee, cupped close in still cold hands. Over breakfast, I pencil out directions for Henry. The rest of our group are intent on pushing on to Santiago. After a second cup, we say goodbye, and I walk through town to the train station.

Two hundred metres from the station the level crossing closes. Cars queue before red lights. I walk faster, but then the train arrives, and I start to run, backpack and all. Just as I reach the carriage doors, they close, and the train starts to move. I frantically press the button. Nothing. I wave, to someone, anyone. Then, to my surprise, the train stops again and the doors open.

Breathless, I take my seat. As the guard approaches, I can only motion a running action. 'Yes, I know,' he says.

Thirty minutes later the train slows into Santiago, disgorging a flood of pilgrims from Eastern Europe, America, Spain.

Chapter 11

Santiago de Compostela

I walk uphill to the Plaza de Galicia and into the cathedral quarter. Everywhere, the clack of walking poles, tapping out their codes of arrival, a chorus line set for their finale in this sing-song city.

Again, umbrellas raised high, across a side street off Rua Nova; in rows of red and yellow, strung from balcony to balcony in a blaze of what must be this season's, or rather every season's colours: the burnished red and saffron of the Spanish flag, of generosity and courage, of Camino arrows and scorched skin.

Further along Rua Nova, I come across a place called Pilgrim House. Curious, I wander inside to a smiling welcome from an American woman who married a Spanish man. She explains that they are a non- profit initiative. 'Pilgrims can leave their backpacks here while they explore, or grab a coffee, talk to someone. Our vision is a place for respite and reflection.'

To aid this, they offer gatherings twice a week and a guided meditation, a sort of Lectio Divina, she says, giving a chance for pilgrims to discuss, share their stories, experiences, in community.

I grab a coffee, sit in the peace of their library for a few minutes and check their website. It says, 'We go through times of joy and deep thankfulness alongside times of loneliness and maybe even darkness. This is simply the nature of being human. Pilgrim House is a place away from home that is full of souls sharing in all the uncertainties and celebrations of the journey. For, are we not all wandering?' For such generous words and genuine hospitality, I feel grateful.

I leave my backpack there, then walk up to the Pilgrim Museum where I've arranged to meet Thomas. Someone taps my shoulder from behind.

He stands back. 'You lost the beard then?'

'Yes, it came off at Vilanova. Far too warm for it.'

'This walk, it did you a power of good,' he says. 'I can see that. I stayed in Muxia for a couple of days and wandered all around the coast.'

'Well, did you enjoy?'

'It was beautiful on that causeway in front of the church. Those giant stones with the waves breaking over them.'

'As they have for thousands of years,' I say.

'I found the exact spot where Martin Sheen's

character scattered his sons' ashes at the end of *The Way* – into the ocean. It makes you think.'

We sit down in a café and exchange our stories, he of the people he met en route and in Muxia, then I, searching for the words that could explain something of the wonder of the Stone and Water route. He tells me that with this trip, he may have got the Camino out of his system.

I say it's too late. 'You'll never get it out of your system.'

He laughs. 'You may be right, but I can't tell my wife that. I don't have the words.' He has been here all morning and seen everything, again. Then he tells me, 'You have a wander round. Take your time, visit the cathedral. It's important. I'll see you out at the airport, in a couple of hours.'

Exhilarated, relieved, and bathed in a sweet melancholy that the walking is over, I amble around the breathless squares towards the cathedral. No sense of anti-climax. There is music everywhere: Spanish guitars play Rodrigo, then Bach and Corelli echo from a mandolin, their notes hanging in the air.

The Jazzman Santiago was still there, all the way from Uruguay to the colonnades of Praza Quintana with his Black Gibson Les Paul, the reverb on his amp set high, drifting out Bossa Nova in bright sunshine. He remains politically incorrect in his

black face-stocking stretched tight, a fake cigarette
butt stitched to the bottom lip of his mask, a white
straw hat on his head. It's as if this were St Louis,
and any minute a paddle steamer might slide past,
barrelling out the Stephen Foster songbook.

*Pilgrims queued across the Praza Quintana, Santiago de
Compostela, for the Puerta Santa, the Holy Door*

I stop to compliment him. 'Bossa Nova. Perfect for a
day like this.' Cool jazz, in a smooth conversation
under summer skies. His chords drift across the
square, to a line queued for the Holy Door into the
cathedral, the ornate Puerta Santa, opened in this
Galician Graceland, in this year of mercy. Some turn
and nod in appreciation.

I move away as he plays Manha de Carneval (Carnival Morning); as the St James re-enactor arrives for his shift; as the Galician Gaita (Bagpipe) player starts to skirl his pipes. The same people in the same places as time goes by.

In the Praza do Obriadoro, the Golden Square, a Babel of tongues rise through the golden air from a collage of arrivals, their dancing celebrations before another set of West Towers, canvas covered in seemingly endless restoration.

On what is now my fifth visit, I stand before this great cathedral, this timeless place of whispers back and forth of another world; its builders obeying the same impulse stretched back 4000 years when people began making their way to votive places, to caves, springs.

Then great tombs and barrows followed, built in places of magical significance, holding the bones of the founding fathers of each new community. It happened again and again, in cycles of building and remembering, until, eventually, the stones became churches, then great cathedrals, celebrating the final revelation.

Threading my way through the crowds, I walk up the staircase and inside to the Portico de Gloria, a high point of medieval architecture, and the place that moves me most. For, dividing the central arch is the Mullion (pillar) where, at its base, the hands of millions stretched their fingers into place, grooved deeper and deeper into marble – as if they'd tried to press right through stone, to the Otherworld.

Atop the column James is seated, leaning slightly forward as if in welcome, his face smooth, serene, raised to rest after his labours, just below his cousin Jesus.

But I'd also been moved by a simpler statue, out in the open air with few visitors except the occasional stray. Twenty kilometres back was the voice of the still small stone James reminding me of my enduring need for the carpenter, the one who put all this in motion, the unlicensed Rabbi let loose again on the highways and byways, sparking new conversations on the way to a Galician Emmaus.

This place is never the same twice. Each time, a different glint of the diamond.

Too late for pilgrims' Mass, I drift with the crowds, circling again in their hajj of wonder. Some stop before statues; I wander into a side chapel and sit awhile.

There, in the dimmed light, votive candles gutter, their reds and whites reminding me of last Christmas, of St Jude's, in Belfast, the church where my parents married; the church to where my father's Dunkirk comrades marched in remembrance. St Jude: the patron saint of seemingly lost causes who told his congregation to hold on, to endure.

In 2016, a year of remembrances, of the Somme, the Easter Rising, and of new shocks, the tide has turned. The Brexit boats are casting off to sail home again across the English Channel, after sacrificing so much, leaving behind only the graves.

I wonder if St Jude has one more miracle in him, for us in Ireland and in Britain, for the tribes from across Europe and beyond, again taking to the road.

It's in times such as these, as the tectonic plates of geopolitics shift, that we look again to myth, for waymarks, guide stones, tracks and trails where others have trod; for how to respond, how to navigate both our inner and outer landscapes. We could do much worse than look to the courage of James – and Jude.

I read again in my journal some of Matthew Henry's comments on Ecclesiastes, that, 'To expect happiness in a changing world must end in disappointment.' Instead, he encourages us to 'seize the favourable opportunity for every good purpose and work. This is given us, that we may always have something good to do.'

I need to find that good.

* * *

I check my watch. My time has run out, my enchantment finally ending.

But what I didn't know as I walked into the bright sunshine, and towards the shortened, dank days of autumn, was that I'd play and replay these last few days, and that steps taken once in time would multiply in memory, my mind hovering over each scene, feeding again and again on each moment; or that I'd seek out the resonance of water racing, listening still for some translation of its angel echoes. Until the seasons turned to spring, and, I'd be drawn to re-join the lines of pilgrims, straggling past the treasure fields, their whispered longing still, for 'once more.'

I descend the staircase and retrace my steps downhill through the crowds. At the Pilgrim House, I collect my backpack and walk through the Porto do Camino.

From south and east, excited faces and tired limbs converge – pilgrims in constant flow, arriving like waves that break on this sandstone city shimmering in the heat at journey's end. One, visibly wilting, asks me, 'How much further to the cathedral?' to where James waits in his gilded palace, in his soft marble.

I point and say, 'Not far, almost there,' then cross the road to Praza Galicia, queue for the airport bus and take my seat.

A girl is about to step onto the bus. A boy reaches for her hand to say goodbye. At arm's length his hold lingers, then, he raises her hand to his lips and lets her go. As she pays for her ticket, stores her backpack, he half paces back, forwards, hands on hips, his tee shirt printed with walking boots beneath the slogan, 'No Pain, No Glory.'

She goes to the folding door. More words are cast on the space between them. They move closer, but the folding doors hiss, and they step back. With her palms to the glass, she mouths, 'I will write.'

I wonder if she will, in this time of gathering stones, memories – in this time to embrace then turn away.

Appendix A

Information and Contact Numbers

Tourism Office Pontevedra
Calle Marques de Riestra, 30 Baixo
36001 Pontevedra (Galicia)
Oficina.turismo.pontevedra@xunta.es
Tel:+34 986850814
Fax:+34 986848123

St John's Monastery Poio
36995 Poio, Pontevedra, Spain
Hospederia Monasterio de Poio:
Rúa Convento, 2, 36995 Poio, Pontevedra, Spain
Tel: +34 986 77 00 00 (Around £40 for a double
room)

Armenteira Albergue is open all year round.
Lugar a Vilar, 53, 36192
Armenteira, Pontevedra, Spain.
Tel +34 670 75 77 77 (Carmen)
During the winter the Albergue was modernised
and re-opened on 30th March 2017. It now provides
32 new bunk beds, a vending machine for snacks
and coffee, a dining room and a small kitchen.

The Cistercian Monastery of Santa Maria – Armenteira

Armenteira 36192.

Tel: +34 627 097 696 or by email:

info@monasteriodearmenteira.es

Albergue Vilanova de Arousa

Pavillion de Deportes, Avenida do Rocheo.

Tel: +34 633 906 490

Upstairs, in the sports centre, part of the first floor given over to an Albergue.

The boat to Pontesecures is booked via the Albergue Vilanova de Arousa. The cost in 2017 will be 19 Euros.

Alfonso and Debee Cherene

Vilanova de Arousa

Cost: By Donation.

Accomodation for six people in their residential annexe.

2 x 3 single beds, with shared bathroom.

Family meals, use of kitchen and house.

email: viaiberia@gmail.com

Whats app: Alfonso Cherene

Cell no +34 650501227

Pilgrim House Welcome Centre
19 Rua Nova
Santiago de Compostela
Galicia, Spain, 15705
pilgrimhousesantiago@gmail.com
pilgrimhousesantiago.com

Youtube video in English for the Stone and Water route
Variante Espiritual Camino Portugues (English)
https://www.youtube.com/watch?v=yHkQ5NpGeFs

Acknowledgements

With thanks to my wife, Kay, for her understanding and support. Thanks also to Kathleen Quinn, for reading the manuscript and for her invaluable advice, to Celestino Lores for writing the preface, and to Alfonso and Debee Cherene for their kindness and hospitality.

About the Author

Roy Uprichard was born in Belfast and, as a mature student, graduated from Queen's University with a BA Hons in Politics and Sociology and an MSSc in Irish Political Studies. Then, for the next twenty-four years, he lectured in Further Education, working with young adults with learning difficulties.

In 2010, in a partially successful assault on middle-age spread, he trekked part of the Annapurna circuit in Nepal. In the summer of 2012 he discovered the Camino Frances. That autumn he walked the Camino Portuguese from Tui and, on his retirement in 2014, returned to walk the entire Camino Frances, recorded in his travel memoir, *Restless Hearts*.

He has since walked St Cuthbert's Way in Northumbria and, in August 2016, the Camino Portuguese from Porto taking the extraordinary Spiritual Variant option, the Stone and Water route through hidden Galicia.

He lives in North Down with his wife and hopes to continue walking and writing.

In the interests of privacy, he has changed the names and nationalities of most pilgrims met during the summer of 2016.

Dear Reader,

If you enjoyed reading this book – or you found it helpful or instructive – please leave a review.

Just go to **amazon.co.uk** or **amazon.com**, enter my name (**Roy Uprichard**), or the book title (**Stone & Water – Walking the Spiritual Variant of the Camino Portuguese**) in the search box, scroll down to **Customer Reviews**, then click on **Write a customer review** and let others know what you think of this book.

Thank you,
Roy

Also By Roy Uprichard:

Restless Hearts
Walking the Camino de Santiago

'An emotional and spiritual journey across Spain.'

In this evocative mix of travel writing and memoir, an Anglican fallen out of love with the Church finds himself drawn to walk the Camino de Santiago, where, deeply moved by encounters with other restless hearts, he begins to find his way again.

Review by the Confraternity of St James, London:

> *'More than a memoir. A reflection on life, belief and non-belief, by one of the many restless hearts wrapped in a temporary pilgrim mantle, seeking to regain their land of lost content. Full of vivid description and capturing those fleeting impressions that bring an experience alive.'*

Some of the 5-star reviews of *Restless Hearts* on Amazon:

> *'I recommend this without hesitation. Packed with details and poetry, it will lift your soul. This beautiful book invites the reader to join in the author's journeys, both physical and spiritual.'*

> *'Would recommend to anyone wanting to get an insight into the Camino both physically and emotionally. Enjoy.'*

'Fantastic book for anybody who has, or indeed hasn't experienced the Camino. You feel as if you too are walking with him, bathed in the sunlight of the experience. The immediate challenges and experiences of the Camino trigger the author's memories of long forgotten incidents so that we have walked through many different layers of history by the time we reach our destination at Santiago de Compostella.'

'Restless Hearts is a book I'd recommend to anyone.There are the poet and the artist's hand in this book. The prose is beautiful, he paints a picture of history, both past and present, both entertaining and informative. The interactions with people along the way, the friendships gained that will last a lifetime. I found the book a page turner and reasonably priced. A great present for anyone with a restless heart.'

'A wonderful account of a personal, spiritual and historical journey. Well worth the read.'

'I loved the mixture of travel writing and memories evoked on the walk, the authors reference to making sense of the past and how the Camino brings to the surface things previously buried or denied. I particularly enjoyed the author's recollections of his early life and his search for information about his father.I feel inspired to do this walk and experience the scenery, the people, the light and the villages along the way. Lovely descriptions of all this.'

Made in the USA
Lexington, KY
24 February 2018